Available books by George Mikes

Boomerang: Australia Rediscovered
East is East
Eureka! Rummaging in Greece
How to be Affluent
How to be an Alien
How to be Inimitable
How to Scrape Skies
How to Unite Nations
Humour: In Memoriam (*in association with Routledge and
    Kegan Paul*)
Little Cabbages
Not by Sun Alone: A Jamaican Journey
The Prophet Motive: Israel Today and Tomorrow
Shakespeare and Myself
Switzerland for Beginners
Tango: A Solo Across South America
Uber Alles
Wisdom for Others

THE LAND OF THE RISING YEN

The Land of the Rising Yen

JAPAN

George Mikes

Illustrated by Zabo

ANDRE DEUTSCH

First published 1970 by
André Deutsch Limited
105 Great Russell Street, London WC1

Printed in Great Britain by
Tonbridge Printers Ltd, Tonbridge, Kent

233 96161 5

Contents

Introduction   7

PART 1   PEOPLE
The Scrutable Orientals   21
Okinawa and the A-Bomb   27
Two Nationalists   36
Mere Imitators   42
The Brutality of Gentle People   46
Authoritarian Democrats   50
The Horror of Responsibility   57
Gewalt Rosa and the Rest   62
Driving   71
Manners   76
Soup and Haggis   86
Beauty and Ugliness   88
Snobbery Japanese Style   97
Ladies and Gentlemen   104

PART 2   THE WAY THEY LIVE
Kanji and Kana   117
Nonsensu   127
The Fragile Giant   133
Paradise   142
Politics   147

Tolerance   155
Kabuki Revisited   161
Tempura Mutantur   168
A Crypto-Matriarchy   172
The Geisha   179

PART 3   PLACES
Tokyo   187
Kyoto   193
Osaka   200
Ryokan   203

Introduction

You'll find me unchanged. And why should I change since I have found the happiness that suits me? I have accepted duplicity instead of being upset about it.

At times one wonders, doubting the facts, even when one has discovered the secrets of the good life. To be sure, my solution is not the ideal. But when you don't like your own life, when you know that you must change lives, you don't have any choice.

Albert Camus *The Fall* (translated by Justin O'Brien)

(1) *How Dare They . . .*

The world has a picture of Japan: men and women in kimonos bowing to one another ceremoniously in the shade of pagodas; voluptuous geisha-girls playing ancient stringed instruments, interrupting their playing only in order to utter a few devastating repartees; embarrassed small men and women, coming from flower-ceremonies and rushing, or rather ambling, on to tea-ceremonies, giggling apologetic-

7

ally and hissing furiously while disgruntled *samurai* commit *harakiri* in the background.

Stereotyped images die hard and there is always good reason for their existence. After all, American businessmen do ride in massive automobiles, smoke gigantic cigars, engage frequently in gun-battles with gangsters and when defeated jump on their fuming stallions to gallop away into the infinite emptiness of the Wild West – usually to the infinite emptiness of Los Angeles or San Francisco. The few Britons who are not actually in the Coldstream Guards, sporting red tunics and bearskins and going about their business (usually some royal occasion) on proud and fussy black chargers, are all bowler-hatted stockbrokers, carrying rolled umbrellas, taciturn, reserved and stiff-upper-lipped, getting out of their Rolls-Royces every now and then to play cricket or plot the re-establishment of the Empire, while their womenfolk in cart-wheel hats, decorated with immense flowers in singularly bad taste, hold heated meetings demanding the re-introduction of hanging or protesting against the maltreatment of British dogs in Japan.

These pictures may be caricatures, but the trouble with caricatures is that they resemble the original much more than we (if *we* are the original) care to admit. Besides, the stereotypes represent permanence, something fixed and unalterable, and we stick to them because we are all – even the most progressive, the most revolutionary among us – extremely conservative; we all resent change because we know that while change is life, change is also death, bringing our own inevitable extinction in its wake. So we resent departures from the Japanese stereotype, we object to the Japanese becoming a first-class industrial nation; and so do the Japanese themselves, who nostalgically try to cling to their kimonos and keep bowing with exquisite politeness before concluding multi-million-dollar deals in computers or the building of automated electronics factories; and they always go to geisha-houses to sign the contract.

The world, of course, suffered its first shock about Japan as early as the Russo-Japanese War; but that event, at the beginning of the century, had its legendary, romantic, David-and-Goliath aspect. It was the victory of the insignificant pygmy over the tyrannical bully whom it was a pleasure to see humbled, so Japan's success fired peoples' imagination instead of frightening them (with the exception of the Kaiser who developed his Yellow Peril theory). Besides, Japan atoned for this victory of 1905 with defeat forty years later, so all seemed well for a while.

But Japan's victory of the GNP (Gross National Product – a phrase mentioned much more often in Japan nowadays than *bushido* was in another era) is a more serious matter than the victories at Port Arthur, Mukden and Tsushima were. Japan has become (according to one way of measuring it) the third industrial power in the world; and the race is not yet over.

Different people react differently to this ominous phenomenon. Some speak, contemptuously, of the fruits of defeat. Defeat – as we shall see in greater detail – certainly had its beneficial aspects; but it also meant starvation, atom-bombs, occupation, humiliation, execution of two former Prime Ministers and some other leaders as war criminals, and long years of horrible struggle and poverty, so it was no unmitigated joy. It is not a fair view of history to state that these cunning Japanese (and Germans), recognising the dangers of victory, deceitfully engineered their own defeat to achieve their war-aims. That's only how it looks today; it did not happen that way.

Others resent the basic injustice of the thing. They do not think only in patterns but also in categories. Some people should wear kimonos, others should wear Western garb; some should be a nation of *samurai*, others a nation of vice-presidents. Similarly, there are victorious nations

9

and defeated nations and both categories – in all decency – should stick to their stations in this post-war era. But the sad truth – and many of us must feel a trifle middle-aged or even elderly as a result of it – is that the post-war era is now over. It may have lasted for a generation, but by the nineteen-seventies we are surely the post-post-war era (and, let us hope, not another pre-war era): a very different epoch in mood, outlook, attitudes, fortunes and misfortunes. We must stop thinking in the outworn terms of World War Two. It is not victory or defeat in that encounter which determines our fate and fortunes, but our behaviour, politics, exertions, wisdom and luck in the last quarter of a century. World War Two may have been the latest of wars; but it is now in our past and consequently part and parcel of our lives, our character, our present (like the Napoleonic Wars, the Crusades, the Norman Conquest, the Peloponnesian Wars) and must take its proper – and admittedly very important – part in history.

Others again go to the other extreme. They feel guilty (particularly because of the A-bombs) and ashamed of being the products of European civilisation. They welcome the emergence of modern Japan and look forward to the emergence of modern Africa, rub their hands with glee and await with malicious joy their own destruction.

It is easy and comforting to feel a guilty European (a 'European', somewhat incongruously, means American, Australian, etc as well). It is equally easy to remain an unrepentant European and come back from the Far East convinced of the superiority of our ways. They are indeed superior in many respects, partly because they are better suited to the rotten, automated, money-grabbing society we have built and partly because they are indeed the best by any standard. It is easy to acknowledge virtue in others and belittle ourselves: admitting our weaknesses is simply another way of asserting our moral superiority. For many people it is easier to give than to receive; easier to acknowledge their own guilt than to blame others. About half of humanity is masochistically minded and this way of thinking suits and satisfies this half. It is more difficult to accept our own virtues; to beat – however reluctantly – our chests and to do it without conceit. We Europeans have, after all, achieved a great deal and we might as well give a graceful bow and accept some praise – without humility, because humility is one of the most repulsive virtues, nearly always false. But while admitting our undeniable excellence, we should also reflect upon the fact that our present predominance in many fields is due as much to historic and climatic factors, including an element of sheer luck, as it is to our outstanding qualities; and, in any case, it is only temporary, as was the hegemony of Babylon, Sumeria, Egypt or Greece. Our victory in the Battle of Electronics may prove as ephemeral and evanescent as our victory in the Second World War or as the victory of the Greeks at Marathon. But there is no need to think in terms of victors and vanquished; in terms of *we* and *they*. If humanity – Europeans, Africans, Asians and all – were just a shade more intelligent, we could be victors all; we could be all *we*.

In Japan something is happening now which happened in India some time ago: a new culture, a new way of life is being superimposed on the old one. An alien culture is being superimposed on the indigenous.

'You can't superimpose one culture on another,' people are fond of saying. 'The result is bound to be a mongrel.'

Quite. But what is wrong with mongrels? Of course, a mongrel is neither one thing nor another, neither an Alsatian nor a fox-terrier, but this is no final condemnation. The mongrel is still a dog – with eyes, ears, feelings, passions, jealousies, frustrations and joys of his own. He may be more intelligent, more sensitive and altogether worthier than either of his inbred, aristocratic parents. The verdict: 'He is not a pure-bred Alsatian,' is dismissive and debunking only in the eyes of pure Alsatians who firmly believe that being pure Alsatians is the supreme virtue until they are taught the facts of life, usually in the hard way.

Two superimposed cultures make little sense if they remain separate and unamalgamated. If they can integrate, they produce something new. The whole, after all, is more than the sum total of its ingredients, just as a motor car is more than a heap of spare parts.

The Japanese have not achieved this integration yet and the process seems to be slow, but if they have a genius for anything, it is for imitating others *and* improving on their ways. And as for our own pure-bred Alsatian culture... our Mediterranean - Nordic - Central - European - Slavonic-American culture: there is nothing pure about that. It is a hotch-potch – and it is all the better for it.

We are inclined to think that our ways are the best. Often they are. But here is a sobering throught.

On November 12, 1946, the *Stars and Stripes*, the daily paper of the American army of occupation, arranged a competition in Tokyo between the abacus, still in almost universal use in Japanese shops and offices, and the most up-to-date electric calculating machine, as the budding computer was then called.

'The machine age took a step backwards yesterday,' reported the paper next day. 'The abacus, centuries old, dealt defeat to the most up-to-date electric machine now being used by the United States Government. The abacus victory was decisive.'

I, too, had a memorable experience of a slightly different kind. I went to buy a number of small items in the shop of my Tokyo hotel. The lady in charge took her abacus and I took my little pocket-calculator (I am very bad at figures, so I use a little adding machine, the reverse side of which is a slide rule).

'235 yen,' she declared, looking up from the abacus.

'Surely not,' said I politely, studying my machine. 'You must not cheat yourself. I make it 645.'

'No,' she shook her head, smiling. 'You must not overpay me. It *is* 235.'

Then someone who could do figures in his head came in and told us, quite rightly, that the correct sum was 415 yen.

A simple little story, but for me it has a symbolic significance. This was a clash – however minor – between Eastern and Western methods. We both know that our own method can frequently be right; the wiser among us also know that our method can sometimes be wrong and the other can be right. This little story should remind us – a useful reminder indeed – that we can *both* be wrong at one and the same time.

(2) *Success-story*

How do the Japanese look at all this? They are complicated people. Yet they are also very simple – almost primitive – in one respect: they idolise success. What succeeds is good; what fails is worthless.

Perhaps we are all inclined to think this way, but the Japanese definition of success seems over-simple. Success is what achieves immediate and tangible results; success shines and dazzles, it is there for all to see and can be recognised at a glance. Success is the accomplishment of an aimed-at end – there is no need for philosophical or psychological examinations of the value and quality of aims. Success is fame, status, riches.

This adulation of success has played a dominant part in Japanese history throughout the ages; it formed the

Japanese character; it made world history.

In 1637, after a bloody revolt, the Shimbara Uprising, Japan was hermetically sealed off from the outside world. It created one of the many Iron Curtains of history, much more savage and effective than Stalin's was at the height of his paranoia. No Japanese was allowed, under pain of death, to leave the country, and any Japanese who was foolish enough to return from abroad was executed in a rather unpleasant manner. Foreigners were not permitted to enter the country at all; if they did, they were beheaded.

In 1640, a band of brave but foolhardy Portuguese appeared, bearing presents and hoping that the *shogun,* Iemitsu, might relent. He did not. The whole crew of the Portuguese boat – with the exception of thirteen people – was beheaded; the vessel with its cargo, including all the gifts brought to the *shogun,* was burnt. The thirteen survivors, after witnessing the executions, were sent back to Macao. Before they departed they were addressed, so it is said, by an official in these terms: "You are witnesses that I even caused the clothes of those who were executed to be burned; let them (the citizens of Macao) do the same to us if they find occasion to do so; we consent to it without demur. Let them think no more of us; just as if we were no longer in the world." '*

The rulers of Japan had many reasons for trying not to exist to the outside world, the main reason being the usual fear felt by tyrants: the dread of contamination by a freer spirit. As long as the tyranny was successful, the Japanese, as usual, acquiesced; the country remained isolated, cut off from Western science, progress, ideas. By the middle of the 19th century, the Tokugawa *Shogunate* – essentially a military dictatorship which ruled Japan for two centuries, using the Emperor as a puppet – was tottering. Its fate

---

* Richard Storry: *A History of Modern Japan,* Penguin Books.

became sealed when Commodore Perry opened up Japan to the foreigners. In Japan no régime – not even an otherwise strong dictatorship – could survive such a loss of prestige. After this complete reversal of policy, many other nations would have sulked, turned inwards and developed numerous chips on their shoulders – as indeed the Chinese did. The world treated the Chinese abominably and even many of Mao's determined opponents must applaud his successful restoration of China to full sovereignty; yet the silly and largely unjustified conceit of the Chinese has done as much harm to them as the greed and rapaciousness of foreigners. The Japanese reacted very differently. They said: 'If the *gaijin* (the foreigner) can force us to do things we do not want to do, then the *gaijin* is stronger and more successful than we are. The *gaijin*, indeed, must be better. So we must learn his ways, we must learn all he can teach us. If the *gaijin* has steamships we have never seen before – then we must learn how to build steamships. And then we can face the *gaijin* on his own chosen ground, with his own weapons.' And they did, in almost no time. It is hard to believe that Perry forced the doors of Japan ajar little more than a century ago.

When fascism seemed to be successful, fascism was good and Japan became fascist. When the fascist and militarist war-leaders were hanged in Japan, their execution created less of a problem than the Nuremberg trials did in Germany. There was no sympathy for them – people were thoroughly bored by their trials. They had failed – so what did they deserve? There was no moral indignation in Japan. The Japanese were not outraged either by the guilt of their war-leaders or by the behaviour of the Americans who hanged them. The whole affair lacked moral context completely: it was a question of achievements, not a question of morality. The Americans had full justification – full moral justification, if you like – to do as they pleased: they were the victors. The Japanese generals had lost the war, that made them guilty. Defeat was a traumatic experience; but the execution of the former leaders of the nation was no part of the trauma.

Democracy was victorious, so democracy must be good; let's try democracy. So now the Japanese are trying it with earnest devotion, as they would try anything. If they are told that a sense of humour is a desirable proclivity, they will form serious study-groups to discover how to acquire a really robust sense of humour. There is no hypocrisy about their democracy. Democracy has no intrinsic value in their eyes: democracy is expedient, not a sacred religion. Indeed, they more or less discarded their sacred religion, Shintoism, after the war: it bore part of the responsibility for failure.

The Japanese regard Western systems as closed and final until they are disproved. The systems are magic pills: you swallow them and all your ills are cured. For some of them Marxism is the magic pill. They follow Marxist dogma with faithful earnestness. Neither the democrats nor the Marxists are prepared to study – let alone criticise – their creed and try to improve upon it. They do not take notice of what is happening in front of their eyes: they believe what they have been taught. To criticise, to try to improve, and thus to question the validity and wisdom of the accepted creed would go against their deep and inbred respect for authority – one of the cornerstones of the Japanese social structure. The creed is fully and totally valid until it is fully and totally discredited, and then it is abandoned as worthless.

Do I mean to say that should democracy fail, the Japanese would give it up? Yes, that is exactly what I am trying to convey. There are few predictable events in the future but this is one of them. The Japanese are perfectly right, too. There is no intrinsic value in any political system: various systems can best serve various ages and there was a time when even slavery was progressive (it was surely more humane than the indiscriminate massacre of the captured enemy). But slavery as well as feudalism, free trade, protectionism, and diverse revolutionary, fascist and monarchical systems became outmoded and thrown on the rubbish-heap of history. Some Marxists try another old trick nowadays: they try to patch up their own Bible and while paying lip-service to the old giant, Karl Marx, deviate from his ways but call their deviation orthodoxy. So we get Leninism, Stalinism, Trotskyism, Maoism, Fidelism, Tito-ism, the Brezhnev doctrine etc etc, all claiming not only to be better than the others but also to be the one and only True Creed. Democracy is not the one and only True Creed. Its greatest virtue – as Churchill once remarked – is not that it is so good but simply that there is nothing better. As soon as a better system is found, more suitable to the ages ahead, democracy, too, will be discarded. The Japanese will do it without blinking an eyelid; we shall do it blinking many hypocritical eyelids and offering many theoretical justifications.

We gave the Japanese one piece of sound paternal advice: to give up militarism and concentrate on economics. They followed our advice and we find it hard to forgive them for it. The Americans try to persuade them now to revert to militarism – at least to the extent of spending more on their own defence. But the Japanese shake their heads politely and continue to do as they were told. They have given up militarism for good. It makes them virtuous; and also very, very prosperous.

But of course there is no need for anxiety. If success is the hallmark of strength and merit – as indeed it is – then democracy, at the moment, is safer in Japan than anywhere else.

People

The Scrutable Orientals

Japan – there should be no mistake about it – is a lovely and fascinating country and the Japanese are endearing, likeable people. They are kind and courteous; gentle and intelligent; clean and tidy; disciplined and respectful; and industrious, with an insatiable curiosity and appetite for knowledge. They are also proud, ambitious and nationalistic. They are over-respectful towards authority; their individuality – with rare exceptions – is submerged in groups. There are many strongly individualistic groups, like the students, but few individualistic individuals. They can think for others; they can think for the community; but they are not very good at thinking for themselves.

I liked the Japanese more than I expected, although I had visited their country before my present visit and liked them then, too. But I was also disappointed in them. The quaint, outlandish, oriental flavour of the place meant a great deal to me as it does to most occidental visitors. Starting with those lovely complex ideograms, ubiquitous on fast-moving, racy neon-signs. I also remembered the odd and charming formalities of bowing; the equally odd but irksome habit of hissing; the old-world courtesy, the mania for exchanging name-cards. 'Many of these ceremonious habits,' I thought on the plane, flying towards the Land of the Rising Sun, 'are the legacy of the Tokugawa period.

Not entirely, for the roots were grown long, long before that. The ceremonies were instituted and encouraged by the *shoguns* for good reasons: for their very emptiness and pointlessness. The *shoguns* (with quite a few exceptions) were clever chaps and knew that people busy with meaningless ceremonies had little time for political intrigue and conspiracy.'

It is true that the most meaningless ceremonies occasionally led to quite unforeseen complications. One of Japan's great literary works is the *Forty-Seven Ronin,* an 18th-century novel or romantic tale of love and adventure.* A retainer at the Imperial Court, anxious to humiliate a rival, advises him to wear the wrong pair of trousers for a ceremonial occasion. The warrior's humiliation is intolerable; and it demands a horrible vengeance. The story itself is the history of this vengeance, the story of forty-seven brave, avenging *samurai.* All forty-seven are killed before this terrible tale is concluded; villages are pillaged and burnt; countless people ambushed, tortured, massacred; wives sell themselves to brothels to enable their husbands to carry on the fight, etc. All because of the wrong pair of trousers. 'Quaint, quaint Orientals . . .' I thought.

And at that moment a horrible thought occurred to me. They are not quaint. *We* are quaint. Quaint, quaint occidentals.

I thought of a Japanese humorist (in itself a quaint, occidental idea) flying westwards – or perhaps eastwards – to his own Far East, New York, and musing thus:

'I quite like occidentals and their quaintness certainly adds to their charm. I specially like those lovely, odd Roman letters they insist on using, flashing with racy agility on the neon-signs of Times Square and Piccadilly. It's rather

* See also my earlier book, *East is East,* André Deutsch, 1958. I have taken over a few odd paragraphs from the book, without expressing my thanks and indebtedness to myself on each occasion.

exotic and gives one the strongly pleasant feeling of being abroad. And their manners ... their strange ceremonies ... Many of these were introduced by Louis XIV, or by other kings about the same time (although the seeds had been sown much earlier). These European kings (with numerous exceptions) were clever and cunning fellows who knew that people busy with meaningless ceremonies had little time for intrigue and conspiracy. Of course, some of these formalities were not so innocent and meaningless. At least 47,000 people died in absolutely pointless duels. They have a celebrated literary work – *Cyrano de Bergerac* it's called – in which a knight is killed because he made a remark about this chap Cyrano's nose. I shouldn't be surprised to hear that a few of them died because – say – someone gave them the advice to wear the wrong pair of trousers on some ceremonial occasion. How stupid can one get? ... And those quaint occidental habits! ... The Central Europeans keep kissing women's hands; the Germans keep clicking their heels; the English jump up twenty-five times when the same woman returns to the same table where they have been sitting together for hours. And they don't have the elementary good sense to exchange cards when introduced. The result is that the English never know anybody's name and when they do they don't know how to spell it; and the Americans are not above the extreme rudeness of asking: "What did you say your name was?" And, good gracious! don't they have dirty habits? They wear shoes – the same filthy shoes they were wearing outside in the street, treading in God knows what – inside their homes, instead of changing into slippers. They don't change into a comfortable *yukata* either, but keep on their silly clothes; they actually wash themselves *in the bath* – instead of before getting into it – and then sit in their own dirt, feeling proud of their cleanliness; also they have their soup at the *beginning* of a meal. They must be mad.'

Before going to Japan I was warned by many people who
know the country well that one should never ask a straight
question in Japan; if one does, one never gets a straight
answer. Personal questions are even more out than in
Britain. One cannot form friendships, and one cannot even
get on reasonably close terms with a Japanese, and one
cannot – most definitely not – joke with them. A diplomat
who had served in many oriental countries told me that
human relations were almost impossible. 'When I played
golf with three other men in Thailand, we were four people
playing golf; in Japan I always feel this cannot be achieved:
it will always be one European playing golf with three
Japanese.' All these statements pleased me because they
suited my image of the Inscrutable Orient. Imagine, then,
my disappointment when I kept finding interesting, respon-
sive people everywhere I went: openhearted and broadminded men and women, ready to discuss any public or
private problem – so long as they felt that my questions
were prompted by real interest and not by idle or offensive
curiosity. And quite a few of them were amusing and witty.
I found the Japanese extremely scrutable.

This seems to point to the fact that the Japanese are human
beings like the rest of us, but they will strongly resent this
insinuation. They want to be different. They are determined
to be puzzling, quaint, unfathomable and inscrutable; they
insist on being more Japanese than most of us. They don't
always succeed.

Pachinko is one of the post-war manias of Japan. All
large – and indeed all small – towns have several *pachinko*-
halls. *Pachinko* is pin-balls, also called a pin-table: you push
a button which sets a ball in motion. If the ball falls into a
hole, you win; if not, you lose your money. An English
friend told me in front of a Tokyo *pachinko*-hall:

'A Japanese explained to me that *pachinko* was an in-

genious Japanese post-war invention. And little wonder, he said, that the Japanese had invented it because other nations were unfit to play it. The truth was – he went on – that the right thumb of the Japanese was specially constructed, it possessed a certain knack, ingenuity and finesse, completely lacking in other mortals. He was so proud and genuine about it that I did not have the heart to tell him that my grandfather – before the *First* World War – owned seventy-seven of these machines, called in our parts vertical pin-tables, and operated them at an exotic place called Southend. My grandfather made a good living on the English *pachinko*-machines, in spite of the fact that all the people of Southend, not to mention visiting Londoners, seemed to possess specially constructed thumbs and were endowed with a knack, ingenuity and finesse lacking in other mortals.

The Japanese will be seriously hurt by my denying them the quality of inscrutability. An Englishwoman, who taught at one of their universities, told me:

'I was always irritated by this game of "inscrutable Orientals". I met too often with the response: "Oh, you can't possibly get it . . ." Or: "It's no use trying to explain it to you. One has to be Japanese to understand it." I would reply: "You just explain it to me as clearly and intelligently as you can and I will understand it all right." One of my Japanese colleagues smiled superciliously on one occasion but proceeded to explain the matter with exemplary lucidity. "You see," I told him, "I understand it all right." This upset him. He grew serious. "You really do?" he asked me anxiously. "Perfectly," said I. He shook his head sadly: "Then I must have explained it badly." '

Okinawa and the A-bomb

The West has a heavy load on its conscience *vis-à-vis* Japan: the atomic bombs dropped on Hiroshima and Nagasaki; the only two nuclear bombs ever dropped on live targets; two bombs to remind us that in life-and-death struggles nuclear weapons *are* being used. Looked at from the Japanese viewpoint, the atomic bombs take on other aspects: it is not the A-bombs that made a lasting and ineradicable impression, but defeat. The crippling and sobering effects of defeat still reverberate, and its consequences in modern, practical politics manifest themselves – most conspicuously – in the Okinawa issue.

Defeat was as novel for Japan as the A-bomb. She had never experienced either. She was not prepared for the Bomb but, thinking herself invincible, was even less prepared for defeat. It is true that Commodore Perry forced America's – and the West's – will upon the country but that was no military defeat. It was, indubitably, the result of weakness but there had been no war. All Perry did was to deliver a letter from President Fillmore to the *Shogun*, in the summer of 1853, demanding the opening of trade relations, and some coaling rights. He said he would return for an answer next year. Before leaving, he made a show of force by sailing up Yedo (Tokyo) Bay in defiance of the Japanese government. The Japanese had never seen a steamship before and were duly impressed. When Perry returned

27

in February 1854 they capitulated, and a few weeks later a trade and coaling agreement was signed in the fishing village of Yokohama. Japan benefited from this lesson so effectively that half a century later she was able to inflict a resounding defeat on land and at sea on one of the greatest and most dread military powers of the world. In World War One she was not one of the major belligerents but with her navy she was an exceedingly useful ally and was, once again, on the winning side. World War Two began for Japan with her inflicting an all but annihilating blow on the mightiest navy of the world. (She did this without a declaration of war. It is half-forgotten that she did exactly the same in the Russo-Japanese war. Negotiations with Russia had broken down and on February 8, 1904, Japanese destroyers sailed to Port Arthur where they found the Russian warships with lights undimmed. They fired their torpedoes and hit two battleships and a cruiser without suffering any damage. One day later there was a minor, inconclusive encounter between Russian and Japanese warships and *two* days later war was declared. *The Times* commented: 'The Japanese Navy has opened the war by an act of daring which is destined to take a place of honour in naval annals.'* When thirty-seven years later, after the breakdown of negotiations, the Japanese employed the same tactics against the Americans, *The Times* condemned it as a fashionable trick of Axis warfare and quoted Cordell Hull on the last Japanese note, describing it as 'crowded with infamous falsehoods and distortions'.)

In any case, the beginning of World War Two confirmed the legend of Japanese invincibility. Having nearly knocked out the US Navy at Pearl Harbour, Japan advanced and occupied South East Asia including the impregnable fortress, Singapore; sank two British battleships; invaded New

* Quoted from Richard Storry, *op. cit.*

Guinea; bombed Australia; threatened India – and all this with a speed that made the German *blitzkreig* look like a boy scouts' war-game. The Japanese public knew all about the victories; it knew little about the subsequent reverses. When defeat came it seemed even more crushing because it was unexpected.

Japan suffered terribly from the atomic bomb but never adopted a pose of moral superiority, implying: 'We would never have done it!' The Japanese know perfectly well they would have used it had they had it. They accept the idea that war is war; they give no quarter and accept none. Total war, they recognize, knows no Queensberry Rules. If you develop a devastating new weapon during a total war, you use it; you do not put it into the War Museum.

The devastation, horror and inhumanity of the bomb were unspeakable and I am not trying to diminish its effects, but neither am I trying to be frivolous when I say that, in the long run, the bomb had certain beneficial effects on the Japanese psyche. It rid them of guilt. The Japanese are not given to introspection and they were never devoured by feelings of guilt; psychoanalysts make a poorer living in Tokyo then they used to in Freud's Vienna or do in present-day New York. If war entitled the enemies of Japan to drop atom-bombs on them, then they, too, are certainly exculpated from the charges of lesser but nevertheless grave brutalities. The trials of major and minor war criminals, as I have said, aroused nothing but boredom in Japan; if they meant anything, they meant vicarious atonement for the Japanese people. They paid the penalty through the lives of Tojo and the others. (Altogether about nine hundred Asian war criminals were executed in Japan, Singapore, the Philippines and other former occupied territories.) Bills were settled, debts were paid. But if the trials cleared the Japanese people, then the atom-bombs, surely, tilted the moral balance in their favour. They had been wronged;

they became victims; they deserved – they felt – sympathy not condemnation.

But as the Japanese are basically disinclined to regard war as a moral issue, the second effect of the A-bombs is even more important. The atom-bomb was a purely technical invention, like the steamship in an earlier period: then Perry had steamships, the Japanese didn't. The A-bomb once again underlined the technical superiority of the United States. This was acknowledged, even admired. But it had nothing to do with military prowess. The atom-bomb was dropped by the side which *had* it; not by the side which possessed more courage, valour and military genius. But for the atom-bomb Japan would have remained undefeated. In this way the atom-bomb preserves and upholds the belief in Japanese invincibility. The legend of invincibility can thus gloriously survive the most devastating defeat.

The A-bomb was Commodore Perry all over again. It was Perry in a modern, diabolically destructive, twentieth century guise. It was not the only factor which defeated Japan but it was a decisive one. It opened the country up to the *gaijin* in an even more crushing and irrevocable manner than the Commodore had done. Yet, history never repeats itself. It moves in spirals, never in grooves. A century before, Japan had said: 'Very well, let us learn the foreign devil's skill and artifice and beat him at his own game.' Twentieth century Japan still wants to beat, or at least equal, the *gaijin*, but only in the more important economic field.

The third and most important psychological effect of the bomb was a thorough revolution. This revolution is unmixed with moral indignation or self-pity: but it is deep and sincere; it is profound and nation-wide. The Japanese, so ingenious and eager to learn, absorbed the lesson as they saw it: nuclear bombs are not to be copied – as battleships, torpedoes and military devices were in the last century – but avoided as evil. They perceived that no nation will have the choice of being bomb-thrower or target in a nuclear war: participants will be both. Japan is the only nation which knows what it means to be a target in an atomic war. She has had enough of it.

Japan has turned away from aggressive military chauvinism and has embraced a substitute nationalism: economic glory.

Old-fashioned nationalism survives mostly in one issue: Okinawa. This is inevitable. Okinawa touches too many chords in too many hearts and appeals to everyone, from the extreme right to the extreme left. Some people talk of Communist exploitation. Sure enough, the Communists try to exploit the issue but they did not create it. As a choice for exploitation it is perfect: it is the one issue which unites the old-fashioned chauvinists with the anti-American left.

The left, Socialists and Communists alike, want the Americans out and want to harm American interests. But the extreme right, too, wants the Americans out. The post-war era is over, they feel, and as Japan has now become an important economic power, and an equal and trusted partner, war-time conquests and military bases must be given up. The Americans would be quite willing to comply with these wishes: they do not want to retain political sovereignty over Okinawa as long as they can keep the bases – after all, they have nearly a hundred and fifty other bases on Japanese territory and no one ever protests against their existence. But there is a grave complication in the case of Okinawa: it is the most important *nuclear* base on the Ryukyu islands, a vital link in the American defence-chain. The Americans would be quite ready to return the Ryukyus to Japan if they were allowed to retain the nuclear bases; but the Japanese constitution forbids nuclear bases on Japanese territory. The dilemma is simple: if Okinawa is to become Japanese territory it must cease to be a nuclear base; if it is to remain a nuclear base it cannot become Japanese territory.

The Americans are keenly aware of this dilemma. Japanese friendship and goodwill are overwhelmingly important to them and, indeed, Okinawa is the only serious cloud on the horizon. But it is becoming more and more menacing. America also has her own nationalists, her Pentagon and indeed, her true national interests. The conquest of Okinawa cost nearly 40,000 American lives. But even if they do not argue in the terms of war-time sacrifices: today the United States has ninety-one military installations and 45,000 troops on the island. Okinawa is only five hundred miles away from Shanghai – its military importance is obvious – and neither Taiwan nor the Philippines could compensate for its loss. The United States might be ready to remove nuclear bases from Okinawa and agree to consult the government of Japan before operations are carried out against other Asian nations – i.e. to accept the same conditions that operate for the other hundred and forty-eight American military bases in Japan, about which, I repeat, one hardly ever hears one critical word uttered.

The conservative and pro-American government of Japan is in a quandary. Okinawa is for Japan what re-unification is for West Germany: not everyone regards it as a burning issue but no one dares say so; everyone must pay lip-service to its overwhelming importance. The government would like to play the Okinawa issue down but it cannot: it is much too explosive – and elections are not far ahead. The government, one feels, would be quite prepared to accept the American suggestion that they take Okinawa back and change the Constitution – at least so far as this single exception is concerned – in advance, to allow American nuclear bases to stay on. But anti-nuclear and anti-colonial feelings are fierce, and the Japanese public would not agree to receive Okinawa back conditionally or to bargain away the most sacred clause of the Constitution. The discovery in July, 1969, after an accident, that the Americans were stockpiling nerve-gas, a powerful chemical and biological weapon, at Okinawa, has hardly contributed to the calming of passions.

The Okinawans, too, press hard: they want to return to the motherland. Somewhat unwisely, some people maintain. Okinawa, for a while, after the war, was better off than the rest of Japan: the United States forces brought prosperity. Today they are worse off than booming Japan and the loss of the United States army and navy would mean a crippling blow. But nations do not live by bread alone and the wishes of the Okinawans, logical or irrational, must be respected, as the wishes of the Gibraltarians, who refuse to be returned to Spain and wish to remain British, are also respected. Millions of Japanese feel that the shame and humiliation of defeat will not be fully expurgated until Okinawa is returned; the left uses Okinawa as a convenient stick with which to beat the United States; and even Big Business, rarely carried away by emotion or burning with the flame of patriotism, presses for the island's return. A few economists insist that the patriotism of Big Business is not unconnected with Okinawa's economic situation. The island has no natural resources, no industry and after the departure of the American forces is bound to become a source of a great deal of cheap labour.

The Security Treaty between Japan and the United States comes up for revision in 1970 and all concerned – Americans, the Japanese government, Okinawans, Communists, students – are getting ready for a battle royal. And elections are looming on the horizon. There are signs that the Americans are prepared to bow to Japanese intransigence on this issue and regard Japanese friendship (as well as the comfort and interests of a friendly Japanese government) as of greater value than the base. 1972 has been mentioned as the proposed date of return – but only after some tough bargaining. Indeed when Premier Sato visited the United States in November 1969, President Nixon promised him the return of Okinawa in 1972. The islands – according to the President's plans – will be de-nuclearized but they will remain a US base. In certain circumstances they would be used as bases for B-52 raids and in other, properly defined, circumstances, the Americans will have to consult the Japanese government before acting – as in the case of other bases. These American concessions have calmed tempers to some extent and the Japanese government has undoubtedly scored; yet the reservations give rise to some anxiety and dissatisfaction in Japan and the Okinawa affair is far from being closed.

In the meantime, the Americans look with faces both envious and wry in the direction of the Sakhalin Islands. These islands were ceded to the Soviet Union after the war and no one knows whether they are or are not used as nuclear bases. Yet the Japanese Communists (and other Japanese parties for that matter) rarely utter a word about Sakhalin. Stalin expelled all Japanese inhabitants as soon as he took over, so there is no revisionist movement and no Sakhalin problem, while the Americans must pay the price for their own decency and tolerance. Which proves once again that virtue doesn't pay while crime carries within itself its own satisfying, rich rewards. (It was reported that the Japanese Foreign Minister, during his visit to Moscow in September 1969, raised the issue of the Sakhalin islands with his hosts. It was an extremely clever move: it proved that the government was more patriotic than its extremist critics and the issue must become very embarrassing to the Communists. They cannot possibly press for the return of Okinawa and demand at the same time that the Sakhalins be forgotten.)

Apart from Okinawa, Japanese nationalism takes rather innocent forms. The Japanese are competitive people and they want to shine; they want to be first in every field; they want admiration – like the Americans, the French, the Russians, to mention only a few from a long list. The Japanese want to beat the Americans at baseball – a very popular game in Japan (they will never do it due to their smaller build). They want to produce better cars, better photographic cameras, better transistor radios – and they have certainly made pretty convincing efforts here. They want to be victorious in sport, but rarely are nowadays. The great Japanese swimmers of the past are almost forgotten and ping-pong isn't really one of the great games. When Japanese athletes are defeated – in other words, pretty frequently – many Japanese cry. But they can and do proudly claim that they produce more flavours of ice-cream than the United States, that nation hitherto generally revered as the greatest ice-cream nation on earth – and soon on the moon too. But it is in the realm of chewing gum that a happy solution lies: the Japanese have produced a chewing gum with the flavour of *sake*, their rice-wine. As heartening an example of the amalgamation of two cultures as I have ever seen; a glorious feat of uniting the worst of two worlds.

A final thought: Okinawa is a reminder that old-fashioned nationalism is not dead in Japan. A great and proud nation must find a proper outlet for its talent, and energy. Should Japan find such an outlet in the substitute nationalism of motor-cars, cameras, transistor radios, baseball and ice-cream, or in the grimmer type of nationalism hinted at in the Okinawa issue? This is the real question for Japan and the world. It's either-or.

Two Nationalists

Defeat rankles; yet Japanese nationalism is not aggressive. Even in Okinawa, all they want is to get back a purely Japanese island. Japanese nationalism is often bitter, disillusioned and ambitious; but hardly ever aggressive. In this chapter I should like to describe two extreme types of Japanese nationalist: the most sophisticated and the most naïve. The first gentleman quoted is a member of the government. (To be on the safe side I shall not name him although he makes no secret of his views.)

'We are the true isolationists of this world. Our basic desire is – or would have been – to be left alone. A little more than a hundred years ago our country was opened up by force and this, naturally enough, strengthened our nationalism. This nation depends more on foreign trade than any other, with the exception of Britain. We have to import so much oil that our annual import would be enough to cover the whole of Japan with a fifteen-inch layer of oil. Yet we would be happier without the influence of the outside world – and without its oil. Our natural inclination, like the natural inclination of the British, is for isolation. The Japanese are neither travellers nor explorers. From Kyushu you can see Korea. Yet it never used to occur to the ordinary Japanese citizen to go there. Our culture comes from China. We made tremendous efforts to learn written

Chinese; our people (and we had very few illiterates) *wrote* Chinese for long centuries and – essentially – do so today. Yet we never really tried to learn the Chinese language. Neither did we try to go over and visit China. Look at our foreign policy. We have become one of the largest and most important industrial nations of the world yet we have no real foreign policy. As far as it exists, it is a policy of non-involvement – a policy aimed at being left alone. Isolation. At the United Nations nothing empties the debating chamber quite so fast as a Japanese delegate rising to speak, putting on his spectacles preparatory to reading a long string of clichés and platitudes. This is deliberate policy on our part. Do you think we are unable to improve the quality of our speeches, to equal, say, Bulgaria or Upper Volta? We don't want to. This excruciating dullness safeguards our non-involvement. The only positive line taken by our foreign policy is not to offend the United States; in sharp contrast with the now departed General de Gaulle whose only positive idea was to offend them.

'The Japanese are reputed to be poor linguists. They seem to be even worse than they are because deep down they do not really want to learn a foreign language – which means English in our case. And we want to prevent foreigners from learning Japanese. We regard foreigners who know our language as intruders on our privacy. One cannot know a country without knowing its language – and we don't want to be known. We need English, you might say. We do indeed. That's why we have found an excellent solution – a truly Japanese solution: we understand English but refuse to speak it.

'Defeat in war used to be different in Europe. France was defeated by the Germans in 1871 but won the next encounter about half a century later; and after another quarter of a century she won a further bout. We can't do that. We really have finished with militarism, we are sick of it. Some nations have been invaded many times; a few never. We were invaded once. Perhaps twice. Not such a bad record – in any case we have to live with it. We have no intention of being invaded again, or of invading others. We have no intention even of becoming Number One Economic Power. We only want to preserve our way of life.

'When Perry arrived, although we were a highly educated nation, people in Yedo (Tokyo), which was even then one of the largest cities of the world, knew nothing of the very existence of the United States. This may have been unpardonable ignorance yet ours was a happy, satisfying and elegant way of life; looking back on it, it seems a Lost Paradise.

'There was one thing in 1945 which shook us even more than defeat. It was the riches – the appalling, dazzling wealth and technical superiority of the United States. We vowed never to be poor again. We have kept our vow. Many people feel contempt for us because – they think – we have totally surrendered to Western ways, in no time at all. They are wrong. Some people – leaders of economic and business life – did exactly that. Or meant to do it. But for many of us the accumulation of wealth is simply a means to a circuitous return to the good old days of Paradise Lost, the pre-Perry days, their freedom, their elegance. The days when we did not know that the United States existed.

'Westernisation? To some extent it is inevitable. We go to work in Western clothes, use computers and Western methods, but go home, change into *yukatas* and *kimonos* and revert to another way of life. Our way is the shell-fish way. The shell-fish has soft meat inside but a very hard, protective shell outside. The *outward* acceptance of Western customs helps perhaps to preserve our *internal* values. The Chinese did exactly the opposite: they tried to reject Westernisation *in toto* and thought, in their conceit which is their gravest national disease, that they knew better about everything. The result was deadly. I am for Westernisation to a certain degree; a great degree. Westernisation is the only method of keeping to our own ways; today Westernisation is our only chance of remaining Japanese.'

My informant had got some of his facts wrong. It used to be forbidden under pain of death to leave Japan, so one cannot speak of a lack of the spirit of adventure. When they could travel they did so. They visited both Korea and China in large enough numbers, even if not exactly as ordinary tourists. In the Meiji era, innumerable study-groups went abroad. When emigration became possible, millions of Japanese went to countries ready to receive them for a while: the United States, British Columbia, Brazil and Peru. Today the Japanese are the greatest travellers, second in number only to the Americans – and surely more curious, more eager to acquire knowledge and experience than the average American. He is surely also wrong about the Japanese unwillingness to learn English. I do not know what's happening 'deep down' but in certain circles the desire to speak English has become a mania.

These views reflect a clash not only between Japan and the West but between the Japanese business-world and the right-wing, anti-Communist *intelligentsia*. The latter feel that the businessmen enjoy all the benefits of Japan's boom but contribute little to world peace, national culture and the true, spiritual interests of a reborn Japan. Fascinating though these views are, deserving attention, they are hardly more than a voice crying in the wilderness. They represent a nostalgic desire, a rear-guard action and a warning which bustling, busy, thriving Big Business is unlikely to heed. But it is a whisper which is going to persist; and, in the end, it will either die out or become a battle-cry.

I was sitting at the bar of a pub in Kyoto, off the beaten track, where a *gaijin* is still a rarity if not a sensation. I was drinking beer when I became aware of being closely observed by a man sitting next to me on a high stool. After a while he overcame his shyness sufficiently to speak to me. He spoke in broken English. He had watched me drink my beer with obvious enjoyment then asked: 'Japanese beer good?'

'Very good.'

A happy grin.

'Japanese beer better than English?'

'Much better.'

A still happier grin. I thought it a shade too triumphant, so I added: 'But German beer better still.'

He was puzzled and taken aback.

'You just said, Japanese beer better than English.'

'Yes. Japanese beer better than English; German beer better than Japanese.'

Long, thoughtful silence. Then a girl came in and ordered whisky. He watched her drink it, then asked me: 'Japanese whisky better than English?'

'Yes,' I nodded, 'much better.'

Delighted grin. He was elated. Then I said: 'But Scotch whisky is better still.'

Painful silence.

'But Japanese whisky better than English?'

'Much better.'

The dethronement of Japanese beer obviously rankled more than the fall of Japanese whisky. He was still brooding over it. He asked: 'German beer best in the world?'

'No,' I replied, somewhat sadistically. 'Czech beer better still.'

'Small country, Czechoslovakia.'

'Tiny country,' I agreed, 'but excellent beer.'

This was hard on him.

'German beer is not best in world but better than Japanese?'

'That is so.'

He had a few more drinks, perhaps to drown his sorrows. He examined my jacket.

'Japanese textile – better than English?'

'No.'

Painful surprise. This seemed unfair. We had more or less agreed that everything Japanese was better than anything English.

'English textile better,' I declared firmly and by then with a great deal of nationalistic pride.

He, anxiously: 'English textile best in the world?'

'Yes. Best in the world.'

Relieved sigh. That was different. After all, the English who had recently ruled the mightiest Empire man had ever known, were entitled to one first.

Someone ordered *sashimi*, raw fish – unmarinated and untreated in any way. Just raw fish. The inevitable enquiry followed.

'English *sashimi* better than Japanese?'

'No.'

He looked at me suspiciously, obviously waiting for the blow to fall. But no blow fell. Not a word about Scottish *sashimi* or Irish *sashimi*.

I didn't wait for his timid question, but declared myself: 'Japanese *sashimi* best in the world.'

Up to now he had taken no notice of the other people in the bar, but he translated my verdict on *sashimi* for all to hear. National pride was satisfied. We parted friends.

Mere Imitators

Yes: imitators. But not mere.

The necessity to imitate the West was born out of Japan's former isolation. Once the Japanese, after the lesson received from Perry, decided to become a modern, industrial nation, they had only one way of achieving this: to learn the skills of the West.

Today the word *imitation* has a pejorative, almost contemptuous ring in Western ears; in Japanese it is a laudatory term.

The attitude of the West is a survival from the twenties and thirties and is of course understandable. In those years the Japanese just copied whatever they could lay their hands on, with complete disregard of patent laws. The copies made were frequently skilful, sometimes ingenious but always inferior to the original in quality and workmanship. Relying on starvation wages paid to their own workers, and on the stolen patents, they were able to dump a lot of cheap and inferior stuff on the world's markets. Little wonder the West became apprehensive and angry, suspicious and contemptuous.

Imitation – or some of its close synonyms – has a different ring in Japan. In the Meiji period, innumerable study-groups were sent to Europe with the sole, admitted purpose of learning Western techniques and learning them fast. They went to Britain, Germany, France, Belgium, Italy and a few other countries (also to the United States, across the Pacific), tried to pick up the best in every country, take it home and improve on it.

They came to Europe and, after relatively brief inspections, transplanted our institutions wholesale. They copied our dress, and our building methods; they copied our parliaments, our press, our railways, our shipping, our mining methods, our royal courts, our criminal and civil codes, our civil service, our armies and navies, our taxation systems. They copied everything, deliberately and not only unashamedly but eagerly, almost proudly. Many of these institutions – European parliamentary democracy, for example – were in need of improvement; yet it cannot be stated that the Japanese succeeded in improving upon them.

For some time we were very patronising about the Japanese ability to imitate – and, of course, flattered, too. We would go so far as to admit that their genius for imitation was better than third-rate originality. During the period of Dumping we were less pleased. After the last war, we saw their car-models and smiled at their names: Century, Debonair, Corona, Gloria, Skyline, Contessa, etc: all the names were Western imitations and so were the cars. Even today, you can see Japanese Fiats, Japanese Alfa Romeos, Japanese minis. We grew more and more patronizing: let them enjoy themselves, let them copy Western brand names, let them produce their second-rate little cars, this concentration on industry will keep them out of serious mischief. They did continue, they kept the Western trade names for many of their products but – to our surprise and often hardly concealed annoyance – their products kept on improving. A few years after the war people said about Japanese cameras: 'Well, not bad for the price.' Then it became widely known that the lenses were superb, perhaps the best in the world, but the rest – shutters, built-in

43

exposure meters etc – were somewhat inferior. But before long Japanese cameras improved further and gained an excellent, all-round reputation – yet remained very competitive in price. Similarly, we tried out their cars and nodded benevolently: 'Not bad,' which in this exceptional case meant what it should mean: not bad but not really good. We were right: even five or six years ago they were not outstanding. Today they are.

The *Japan Times* has a slogan printed on its front page: *All the News Without Fear and Favor*. Being a good Westerner, I smiled at this at first. It was, of course, a childish imitation of the *New York Times* slogan: *All the News That's Fit to Print*. A mere rewording. And why have a slogan, in the first place? The overwhelming majority of newspapers appear without slogans and (with regrettable exceptions) survive. But after a few days I came to regard this slogan in the *Japan Times* as a prototype of Japanese treatment of imported methods and ideas. Imitation? Certainly. Mere childish rewording? Most certainly not. The *New York Times* is one of the world's great papers but its slogan is arrogant. Fit to print? Who will decide for you and me what is 'fit to print'? Who will censor the news for us, and on what grounds, on the flimsy pretext that it is not fit for us to see? What the *New York Times* meant – and practises – is exactly what the *Japan Times* proclaims: *All the News without Fear and Favor*. No goodwill or admiration could call the Japanese slogan original; no malice can deny the improvement.

So what about imitation? We should remember, first of all, that all knowledge is imitation. The baby learns to walk and talk through imitation; man learnt how to build better houses and how to improve on his agricultural methods because he imitated his neighbour or the neighbouring – often previously conquered – tribes; millions of books from the simpler Do It Yourself kind up to the most complicated treatises instructing us how to build space-craft, teach us how to imitate others. In some cases we call imitation knowledge; in others we call knowledge imitation. The Japanese in their wild quest for knowledge, in their insatiable desire to learn, made the imitative aspect of their learning more obvious than most other people. But all who learn imitate.

Even today: when *we* copy things American we follow the fashion; if the Japanese do it, *they* imitate.

While imitation was sometimes a euphemism for unscrupulous stealing of rights and ideas, in other – later – cases it was a pejorative term for learning. There is nothing wrong, *per se*, in imitation and I think the time has come when we should start imitating the Japanese. There are quite a few things we could learn from them to our benefit.

What? one may ask. Many technical innovations and improvements but those are not what I have in mind. We ought to imitate their courtesy; their respect for privacy (respect for privacy, yes: about lack of privacy see later); their veneration of old age; their loyalty – loyalty to families, firms, all the groups they belong to; their pride in their work; their sense of beauty and their cultivation of it in everyday, trivial things; and also their gentleness.

The Brutality
of Gentle People

The mention of gentleness must have caused many brows to be raised. Gentleness indeed? These people whose brutality was notorious have suddenly become gentle? And we should imitate their gentleness?

After spending some time in Japan, one would still be puzzled but would word the same question differently: how could these smiling, bowing, courteous, gentle people behave with such unspeakable brutality as they did? Because there is no denying it: they did.

It is vaguely connected with their devotion to imitation. Some people try to explain it in this simple way. Every significant event in Japanese history seemed to point a moral. Foreigners could force Japan open? Then – said they – we must learn the ways of foreigners; we must learn How to be an Alien in a gigantic, momentous, historic manner. Victory over China in 1894 and victory over Russia in 1905 were not only victories but also proofs that force was to be trusted, force was a successful means of achieving one's ends. 1945 spelt a bitter and very different lesson but this new moral, too, was drawn with alertness. Yet, the fact remains: in her fascist era Japan imitated the Nazis; the Nazis were bestial and brutal so Japan imitated their brutality, too.

This explanation contains a grain of truth but far from

the whole truth. The brutality of Japanese soldiers was exercised against prisoners of war and the civilian population of occupied lands with relish, and was not simply 'put on' as a result of superior orders; it was not just an act of copying half-heartedly some distant, European original: it came from the heart; it sprang from true, deep-seated convictions.

How? And why?

Let us dispel, first of all, the hostile notion – nursed mostly though not exclusively by Russian propaganda – that brutality was natural to the Japanese and that's how they always behaved: that the Japanese, far from being a sweet and gentle people, are cruel and bestial, and their true nature comes out whenever it has a chance. It is, first and foremost, the Russians of all people who have good reason to remember Japanese chivalry. Perry had one great rival in his attempt to force Japan's gates: the Russian Admiral, Putyatin. The Admiral's ship, *Diana*, sank in Japanese waters after a storm caused by an earthquake. Putyatin and his crew were at the mercy of the Japanese whose country they had tried to humiliate and subjugate. Yet the shipwrecked sailors were treated with chivalry and kindness. Putyatin himself paid tribute to Japanese generosity and related that he and his men received all the assistance and supplies they needed and that winter-shelters were constructed for them *on orders from the Japanese government.** Again, all records agree that during the Russo-Japanese War the treatment of Russian prisoners was exemplary, indeed generous.

What happened, then, to the Japanese who could behave with admirable discipline and kindness in 1905? And who seem, once again, to be kind and generous people today?

* See Dr G. A. Lensen; *Russia's Japan Expedition 1852-5*, University of Florida Press.

Surely, more than just a change of allies? (Japan had, of course, no allies in the Russo-Japanese war itself but had an alliance with Great Britain at the time.)

Part of the explanation lies in the very discipline to which Japanese soldiers were always subjected – even during the time of General Nogi. They had too much discipline. Japan even today (as we shall see in greater detail in the next chapter) is an authoritarian society without an authoritarian government. Children have to obey their elder brothers and girls even their younger ones; women their husbands; husbands their fathers; fathers their bosses; and – before the war – all of them had to obey the Emperor, who was divine. Suddenly these slaves to so many masters, these people who had obeyed all their lives, gained real authority: power over life and death. There is no worse master than the former slave: there is no crueller oppressor and avenger – even if he avenges himself on the wrong victims. One may understand him; one cannot acquit him.

General Nogi in 1904-05 demanded discipline from his troops but taught them chivalry; the officers of World War Two demanded even blinder obedience but taught them the moral code of the Nazis, extolled brutality and called humane behaviour criminal softness. The officers treated their own men with extreme cruelty and they were encouraged, indoctrinated to pass on this inhuman treatment to those in their power. Oppressed minions want to kick *someone*: so long as they can kick innocent victims they feel relieved and this relief makes their oppressors safer. Some natural decency – it could be argued – might have acted as a check. It did not. They were far away from home; they were free of shame. What they did so far away did not really count. The Japanese were not the first people in history who accepted a double moral code: one for their own folk, another for inferior breeds.

Their most savage and evil behaviour was reserved for

prisoners of war. They had been taught throughout all their military career, indeed all their lives, that once they put on uniform and swore allegiance to their divine Emperor, their lives did not belong to them any more; they belonged to the Emperor. They were taught that to surrender, to become a prisoner of war under any circumstances instead of dying with gun in hand was cowardice, much worse than death. But they were human and they would all have preferred to become prisoners and survive rather than to die a pointless death. They never said so; few of them dared even to think so; but this, of course, does not change matters. These people, now in their hands, the allied prisoners, had by surrendering done exactly what they all wanted to do, what they hoped to be able to do when cornered and trapped but could never, never do.

It is your own vices you hate with burning ferocity in others. It is the crypto- or suppressed homosexual who hates homosexuality with a blind passion; it is the unwanted, rejected and ugly virgin who is the most savage and outraged defender of morality. They all – the suppressed homosexual, the rejected spinster and other members of this sorry species – hate those who actually perform what they would love to do, but dare not. You may condemn crime with genuinely strong disapproval; but you will only *hate* the criminal who commits your pet crime. That's why moral indignation is often so revolting.

It was the man whose overpowering but strongly suppressed dream was that of becoming a prisoner of war and thus surviving, who hated other men who had the supreme courage to be cowards (as he saw it). They had a courage he completely lacked. Hence the ferocity of his emotions, the acerbity of his envy, the venom of his hatred. He was not forced to be bestial; he enjoyed it.

Authoritarian Democrats

Japan is an authoritarian democracy; an authoritarian society without an authoritarian government. In many other countries people have been determined to remain free but authoritarian régimes have been forced upon them; contrariwise, a democratic régime has been forced upon the Japanese who want, who desire, who need authority over them – yet preserve their democracy.

In most other countries democracy has tended toward egalitarianism. In the United States and Australia the 'I'm as good as the next guy' mentality is an important social force. The same – and fully justified – attitude of the black population causes one of the gravest crises in the United States. In Britain a feeble socialist movement supported by a reactionary Trades Union movement faces an equally reactionary but much more intelligent establishment. The socialist-trade union combination fights for tit-bit benefits, for large, but in the long run insignificant, immediate gains, yet tolerates an educational system which, so long as it continues to exist, will always divide Britain into two unequal parts. In Scandinavia, mild socialist rule, growing affluence plus an almost universal peasant-background of all the people, produce a near-egalitarian society. But Japan, while a democracy, is not an egalitarian society; it is hierarchical and seems to be content with this state.

Perhaps we are inclined to think a modern industrial society needs to be a shade more egalitarian in order to succeed. But Japan has succeeded better than most of us; and one of her vocations, may be, is to bring East nearer to West; tradition closer to the fast-approaching twenty-first century; to fit together the unfitting and unfittable.

It can be argued that even the United States or Australia with all their chumminess and devotion to informality, are far less egalitarian than they tend to believe or pretend.* But, at least, one can *rise and fall* in these countries as well as in other modern, Western, industrial societies. The doors may not be ajar; but they are not locked.

Until recently it was impossible to rise in Japanese society; to fall was equally difficult. Age-long habits die hard. Japan was for many centuries a hierarchial society and the idea of educating people to accept their lot in life was fostered and propagated with ferocious insistence during the Tokugawa period. Muramatsu points out that during the Tokugawa *shogunate* a child's status was determined by birth: 'One was educated and trained from early childhood to adjust to the prescribed *modus vivendi* and appreciate a way of life in an authoritarian atmosphere. To the extent that the individual was obedient and faithful to his alloted position and was content with his rôle in family and society, he could have personal security.'

Adjustment is the key word. Western psycho-analysts have always tried to *liberate* the individual from his oppressive surroundings; Japanese psychoanalysis (gaining ground slowly) aims at enabling people to *adjust* themselves to the existing social order. Western society becomes more and more oppressive and totally absorbing every year and the idea – justifiably – has been born that you can't be happy

---

* May I, with apologies, refer the interested reader to a chapter on Australian egalitarianism in my *Boomerang* (André Deutsch).

without being a hippy; without revolting against conventions. The Japanese aim, on the other hand, is to produce happy, well-balanced and well-adjusted half-slaves (instead of our unhappy and unbalanced half-slaves). Western psychiatrists have already taken notice.

In the old days in Japan, one's birth determined one's whole life. It even decided the language one was permitted to use. The equivalent of a Japanese cockney was not *allowed* to teach himself Oxford Japanese, or the Emperor's Japanese. Violation of the unwritten yet draconian laws of conformity meant not only ridicule but, possibly, even exile. But as ridicule was regarded as worse than exile, the threat of ridicule was sufficient. Peasants were not allowed to eat white rice or wear silk. Merchants had to live in mean little houses. Members of the lowest orders, the outcasts, were not allowed to cover the floor of their abodes with *tatami*: they had to sit on bare, uncovered dirt. It was a caste society, with everyone fitted into his proper pigeon-hole. Those who obeyed and those who gave orders belonged to two different worlds: it was one's birth solely and exclusively that determined to which world one belonged.

To try to rise was as uncreditable as to sink. The status of families hardly changed in 2,500 years. The Imperial family – supreme and until 1945 divine – ruled for nearly all this time, the present Emperor being the hundred and twenty-fourth ruling member of the same dynasty.

How are things today? Conditions had to change to some extent but the heritage of the long past survives. Your birth still determines your fate, the only difference being that in modern Japan you are born twice.

First in the old fashioned way; your second chance comes when you enter – or fail to enter – a university and/or get a job. There is cut-throat competition for university places, particularly at the top universities. There are people who sit seven or eight times – in seven or eight consecutive years – for their university entrance examination and begin their studies (or give up hope) at the age of twenty-five or even later. To get into Tokyo University or one or two of the other top institutions means that you are comfortably settled for life. Huge corporations will vie for your services and the door to high civil service jobs will be wide open. If in Britain the old school tie assures certain atavistic privileges, at least it covers only your chest; in Japan it wraps you up completely for the rest of your life.

I said that the great step was to 'get in' to a University, not to get out, to graduate. The phrase was carefully chosen. He who gets in will get out and graduate all right. It is murderously difficult to secure a place – the entrance exam being the hardest of all; the rest is child's play. Once in you have few problems. Your failure would be the failure of the selectors and that would never do. It is the same with jobs. Once a young Japanese gets a job, he is settled for life. He has to kick his boss down the stairs to get fired. He will be promoted automatically according to his seniority: it does not really matter how well he has worked, only how long. Many offices and ministries are staffed with ageing, inefficient men occupying high positions in their sixties and seventies. Retiring age is as low as fifty-five, but many people leave and take *new* jobs at fifty or so and then serve on, indefinitely.

Discipline survives. It survives in the family; it survives in one's professional life. Humble and submissive respect for the father is inculcated from the earliest possible time. The mother does not count for much as far as respect is concerned, but she is loved and it is she who spends most time with the children. The father, in many families, remains a remote figure, hardly seen – not even after business hours when his duty may take him to a geisha-house or some other place of entertainment. He remains the aloof and silent authority, as the divine Emperor used to be. Japan is more or less a one-parent society. Even babies' heads are pressed into a respectful bow when father appears. Obedience and self-effacement are taught from the child's first week on earth.

The marriage game, too, is overwhelmingly important. Of course, more and more young people marry in the European way: they choose their own partners. This, however, is still much more the exception than the rule. Marriage may be, indeed, the third birth given to some lucky youth: another chance to rise. An eligible, able, good-looking young man, working for a large, even a giant, company may be discreetly informed that he has been chosen as a possible candidate for marrying the Big Boss's daughter. That means that he is one in a field of six or eight. He knows that he is being watched closely, mercilessly and incessantly. His past, his background, his family, his parents' history, his school-life, his former male and female companions will be minutely scrutinised, weighed up and analysed – in a manner which would be tolerated in no other free country. All this, by the way, has nothing to do with the police; in Japan the obtrusive Secret Police is a strictly private enterprise. If the candidate does not drink or gamble, does not start affaires with bar-maids and typists, does not commit any *faux pas*, then he may reach the semi-finals, the finals and, in the end, one of the runners will win. He has to be outstanding *and* lucky. His final success will depend on many factors, except one: the choice or preference of his would-be bride.

If he is not to marry the Big Boss's daughter, there are many minor bosses in the company. In any case, he will be well advised to marry someone connected with his firm. His life belongs to the company. He will be looked after and promoted, he will receive innumerable benefits (more of this later) but he must be loyal and devoted. He must not even take all the holidays due to him. He has – as soon as he reaches a position of responsibility and often even long before that – to give up his holidays voluntarily, except for a day or two here, or a week there. *Majime ningen* is the name for the serious-minded person and one's ambition must be to be regarded as such if one really wants to get on well. (*Well,* I repeat, because once engaged, one will get on after a fashion in any case.) The serious-minded chap goes to the office early, leaves it late, goes out on company business with various clients after office hours and if he happens to be free of clients, he still does not go home to his wife and family, but spends his free time with his colleagues and immediate superiors. Eventually he marries a girl from the company, lives for the company and dies in, perhaps for, the company.

One more peculiar duty: he will have to go to the airfield or the railway station on many occasions, whenever the Big Boss or the Small Boss leaves. Every day at Tokyo station you see large groups – twenty or thirty people – bidding emotional farewell to a man who is going on a routine weekly visit to Osaka, three hours away, to return next day. People bow deeply and run a few steps after the train. Shedding of tears is optional.

In the United States it is still possible to work for a boss for twenty-five years, to be paid off on a Friday and to be told that one's services won't be required on Monday. Such treatment of an employee is unimaginable in Japan. Entering into an employer-employee relationship is like a marriage in Europe, except that it is much more solemn and much more lasting. The job is sacred; and it is meant for life. The bond is indissoluble.

Loyalty is the supreme virtue. The company requires undivided loyalty and gets it. Yes, it gets it, because the relationship is mutual and unlike Western firms the company also gives its devoted – if not unselfish – loyalty to the employees. They are housed (if unmarried), receive comparatively small salaries but stupendous expense accounts, often travel free to work and home – in higher positions their cars will be huge and chauffeur-driven – get subsidised lunches, sporting facilities, holidays, long trips abroad (without their wives) and vast bonuses twice a year. The higher executive gets a house – often rent free – which becomes his own on retirement. His membership to costly and exclusive clubs will be paid for him; he can patronise ruinously expensive geisha-houses and restaurants. Japanese employees are married off, entertained in their free time, looked after in many other ways, treated in illness, pensioned off and buried, never fired.

Respect for authority and self-effacement becomes second nature. The Japanese are so disciplined that even inmates of lunatic asylums – who may have been driven into the institutions by voluntarily submitting to too much discipline – can be ordered about and disciplined by words alone. A patient may imagine that he is the Emperor but he will do as he is told. The Japanese, being human, can be as mad as the rest of us; but violent patients are extremely rare. In other countries this almost blind respect for authority would be subservience; in Japan it is regarded as a virtue. It is the virtue of loyalty, first given then, in later life, received. It is also adjustment; coming to terms with the world and with your place in it. This is how the Japanese individual sees it; Japan as a society also insists on this loyalty and obedience. Other countries may deify change; Japan wants – above all – stability.

The Horror of Responsibility

A short while ago, I read a lament by an American journalist about the slow disappearance of single items from the American market – mostly super-market. You can't get a tomato any more: you must buy three tomatoes wrapped in cellophane; you can't get an ear of corn, you must buy a package of three. You can't get even a can of beer (he says), only a 'six-pack' carton of beer. The advertisers call it an 'easy-to-carry-six-pack', suggesting that it is all for your convenience because it is so much easier to carry six than one.

The Japanese have acquired many ideas from the Americans; the Americans might have taken this one from the Japanese. The Japanese – like American tomatoes – prefer to go in groups of three.

Japan is a country of groups. It is an overcrowded island and groups form naturally, of necessity. Privacy as we know it is unattainable. You cannot have a room to yourself. And if – miraculously – you get one the whole family can still hear you move about behind the thin walls, they will hear every step you take, every sneeze, moan and sigh. Japanese life has extinguished not only privacy but also the desire for privacy. Privacy is equated with loneliness and loneliness is the utmost horror.

The individual has slowly merged into groups like the

American tomato, and is wrapped around by protective cellophane. To push yourself as an individual is invidious; to be ambitious for your group (firm, regiment, university, fellow-students, country) is creditable. For an individual it is still difficult to rise but groups can rise and fall. Business-men – merchants – used to belong to one of the lowest castes, now they form one of the highest; the prestige of the military – the heirs of the *samurai* – is not what it used to be. The group-mentality is as universal in Japan as the cult of the individual is in Britain. Their national sport is the noisy crowd-game of judo: two people in combat but also locked in an embrace; the lonely long-distance runner is not their man.

We Westerners jump to the conclusion that this group-mentality produces, or is produced by, an avoidance of responsibility. We are very nearly right. There is a horror of individual responsibility in Japan, engendering compli-cated and subtle techniques for avoiding it. It is no good rushing to the almighty President of a company even with the most valid complaint and asking him to order his under-lings about. He will not do it. He may take the final deci-sion in all cases, but only after a consensus has been reached. Not simply after listening to various views, but after reaching a genuine and general consensus. (The most important man, the key-man in many Japanese organisations is often a young man who knows the ropes, who knows how to get the necessary approvals in the right order and manner.) Japanese life – social, political, business – may be an oligarchy but it tends to become a meritocracy and a democracy. Gentle or not so gentle persuasion may be backed by authority, pressure, forceful arguments; yet it still remains persuasion and not a high-handed order one *has* to obey. One has the feeling that one is obeying one's own order to some extent, that one shares in the responsi-bility. The President will never tell his directors – or the

board, the salesmen and clerks – that it has been decided to open a new plant in Yokohama. He will ask the others what they think of opening a new plant in Yokohama. As the suggestion comes from the Boss, as a rule everyone will think it a magnificent idea. Even the almighty *pater familias* will not announce that the family will now move into a larger house; he will ask all members of the family how they feel about moving into a larger house. In politics the opposition often complains about the 'tyranny of the majority' which means not only that they have been voted down but that it was unfair to put the question to the vote at all. It is unfair, they feel, to use large numbers as a bulldozer and indeed, minorities should be respected; but the Japanese hate the very idea of voting. Their ideal is to thrash things out and come to a compromise in which all participate and concur. The majority, on the whole, accepts this. This attitude does not only express a respect for democracy, but is also a prudent way of sharing responsibility. Should things go wrong at a later stage, no one can ever pin responsibility on one single person, be he the President of a company or the Prime Minister. Nothing is anybody's responsibility; everything is a joint venture.

This may not always be the most efficient way of doing things but it is not an unwise one. Even groups do not bear full responsibility but are often guided by other groups. The Emperor used to be omnipotent in principle. In practice he was only a figurehead during the Tokugawa period, and always – even after the Meiji Restoration – he had to listen to various groups who really ruled the land. The government of Japan was never as all-powerful as some other governments. Japan for ages has produced no Hitler, no Mussolini, no individual dictator of any kind; indeed, not one single truly prominent politician. Groups, however, have always been painfully apparent. From 1931 (the Manchurian 'incident') to the end of the war it was the military who ordered about an often unwilling government and a most reluctant Emperor; today it is the *zaibatsu* (the powerful business clique – a group, once again, not dominated by any individual) who offer their forceful advice and guidance to the government. The government in Japan, a country where permanence is one of the greatest virtues, is at a disadvantage, being non-permanent; while the army or the *zaibatsu* are permanent bodies.

These ideas – the Japanese feel – do not clash with modern notions; indeed, they create a new Harmony in an unharmonious world. Harmony – in the Buddhist conception – is the Supreme Good. Group decisions, collective wishes, eliminate discord, jealousy, envy. Well, perhaps they don't. It may be slightly naïve to relate Buddhist Harmony to modern electronic industries. But such an idea, once again, reflects our Western smugness. Perhaps it is not so ridiculous after all, even for modern electronic and suchlike industrialists, to recall, however faintly, that certain spiritual values always lurk in the background.

Gewalt Rosa and the Rest

Japanese society looks more homogeneous than any other but, of course, no society of a hundred million people – indeed, no society of any size – is ever homogeneous. As a result, when the surface of strict, almost universal discipline is broken, when the unruly instincts and emotions held down by the discipline erupt, they will do so with volcanic force, with white-hot fury. Modern Japanese society has two main outlets through which violent undercurrents can rise to the surface. The first of these is student violence.

Japanese universities are in an even worse mess than most others. The famous French student riots of 1968 caused much more violent vibrations in the political seismograph but lasted only a fortnight or so. The main universities of Japan have been closed for months and although some limited tutorial and seminary activities are carried on, there is little hope of reopening quite a few of them in the forseeable future. Out of 3,000 institutions called, somewhat liberally, institutions of higher education, a hundred and sixteen have suffered, and they include some of the greatest and most renowned seats of learning, Tokyo and Kyoto universities among them.

Reading reports of student unrest and violence, one keeps coming across the word *zengakuren*. This is a portfolio word – of which the Japanese are very fond – a concoction from the Japanese name of the National Federation of Student Self-Government Associations. Nearly all students automatically become members of it. Some opt out either to dissociate themselves or to join opposing right-wing organisations, such as the Japan Student League, or some breakaway socialist faction. Demonstrations started modestly and meekly enough, on a 'we-too-must-do-something' basis. Then the Cohn-Bendit riots in Paris gave new impetus to the militants and their activities became more vociferous and riotous. The police at first reacted with surprise bordering on amusement. The steel-hemelted rioters were treated with indulgence; 'They're only kids' the police implied. Then, occasionally, one of the kids picked up a stone and bashed in a policeman's head. The police were astonished, pained and became tougher. More and more severe sentences were meted out by the Courts – some students are imprisoned for years – and this real or imaginary injustice inflamed passions and inspired more numerous, more violent and more self-righteous outbreaks. These activities culminated in the ugly violence in the Shinjuku district of Tokyo in October 1968 and in the ludicrous, stark naked anti-Expo demonstrations in Kyoto, in July 1969.

For some mysterious reason *gewalt* – the German word for force – has been taken over, perhaps straight from Marx, and *gewalt* has become a deity in its own right; *gewalt for gewalt's sake* is approved by most militants, as if *gewalt* were always good. It is also abhorred and considered incomprehensible by the establishment, as if *gewalt* were always wrong.

Some students fight for nebulous aims. A few explained to me that they fight against police brutality. When I pointed out that this could not have been their original purpose because student demonstrations had engendered police brutality and not *vice versa*, I was told that, whatever its origins, police brutality was a feature of life now and must be opposed. Others demanded a bigger and better *zengakuren*, but I failed to elicit any reason for this. Surely, a simple change in the size and quality of the *zengakuren* would cure few ills. There is a notorious and fiery fighter among the most militant students, nicknamed Gewalt Rosa – Rosa being a reference to Rosa Luxemburg – a most incongruous cognomen for a Japanese lady of twenty-five. Several professors complained that Miss Gewalt had hit them and kicked them. She declared publicly: 'Instructors are the greatest criminals.' Presumably Gewalt Rosa fights to rid universities of instructors.

The confusion is great and a great many people do their best to add to it. It is very seldom that one can see the students' own case properly and fairly stated in any newspaper. Student leaders can rarely – if ever – speak for themselves or put their own case fairly and squarely in the columns of the commercial press. The riots are good paper-selling news but they are followed by little sympathy and understanding, consequently newspapers, on the whole, make fun of the students and try to show them up as immature fools. Immature they may be; but they are no fools, indeed, some of the leaders are brilliantly intelligent.

The Socialist Party utters the usual pious trash, declaring that while it sympathises with many of the students' demands it condemns violence. Anarchist groups declare that while they do not sympathise with any of the students' demands they approve of violence. Professors look at all the phenomena with more sorrow than anger. They do their best to bring about peace; they talk to these young men and endeavour to make them see the light in the same way they see it themselves; they listen to protests, they argue and they have the students' true interests at heart. They thought they were respected and liked – and so they were, in many cases. So now they are deeply hurt when their goodwill and efforts are met with derision and rebuffs.

The phrase one hears most often is: 'They don't even know what they want!' Professors point to the unholy confusion with a feeling of sad triumph as if this very confusion was the final, conclusive argument; they never try to penetrate it, to understand, to disentangle. Confusion is abundant all right; but it covers under its vast and ragged blanket something coherent, synthetic and intelligible.

It was repeatedly pointed out to me that the militant students are few in number and that a small minority makes studying difficult or impossible for the overwhelming majority, who resent them. This is true: the role of vociferous and militant minorities is the subject of many studies in social science. Some of the big firms – to single out one group – pick up promising young men and girls of peasant and working-class origin, employ them on a part-time basis and send them to universities, at the firm's expense. They would never have reached a university without this help and their main concern is to get on with their studies. They, among many others, are furious with the instigators of the riots. It has been stated that of the 40,000 students at Tokyo University there are only three hundred and fifty activists, and some of these are not students at all. On occasions, so-called students of thirty-eight or forty have been apprehended by the police. I was also told many times that right-wing groups fight left-wing groups, Maoists fight pro-Soviet groups, various socialist factions fight other socialist factions and that, indeed, there are so many shades and cliques, internecine tussles and scuffles, that it is impossible to speak of a 'student movement'. Only love of violence unites them.

It is quite true that there are many shades of political opinion among them: pro-Soviet, pro-Mao Communists (Chinese influence is, of course, very strong and the Chinese example of anti-Americanism has made a great impression); there are many shades of nationalists and most of them, as well as the Communists, Maoists and anti-Maoists, re-

c   65 gard the return of Okinawa as their primary aim. There are some Freudist-Marxist-Leninist groups and other even odder combinations. Some want to end the Vietnam war; others rebel against the older generation, though not in the German manner. Their reproach is not 'Oh, how *could* you do it?', the stricture of German youth; they feel that because the older generation failed, it is useless and has therefore nothing to teach them. The older generation, in turn, refuses to listen to immature youth. It has never been the forte of the elders of Japanese society to listen to their juniors. Today they would not understand them even if they listened. 'They never had it so good' – as a well-known Japanese saying has it – so what do they want? Many students want to get rid of the present government; of the Americans; of the establishment. A considerable number want university reform, and indeed the system is not only silly and outmoded but also corrupt. Too many factions want too many, often contradictory, things and these, in the view of many professors, cancel one another out and turn student demands into nonsense. Others point out in despair that many of these demands have nothing to do with them. University authorities could, possibly, reform the system of entries; but how could they end the Vietnam war?

'They only want to *destroy* and they have no idea what to put in the place of the destroyed institutions': I have heard those words from professors scores of times.

Sometimes I replied: 'But don't you agree, Professor, that if someone is genuinely convinced that something is evil he will try to destroy it? He will regard the destruction of evil as a positive step forward. Don't you see that in such circumstances he will regard destruction as constructive?'

Constructive destruction? They looked at me as if I were either a dangerous anarchist agitator or an equally dangerous madman.

Japanese students – or a small but important section of them – are in revolt against a system, against society, and above all, against a future which they regard as bleak and distasteful.

Their *aim*? They aim at themselves. They want to release themselves from the tyranny of the established order; they seek humanity in a changing, electronic society travelling, as it were, in space and eager to reach the repulsive barrenness of the moon. They seek beauty and goodness in a world where people are not evil, perhaps not even indifferent to these notions, but too busy to care about them. They seek freedom: not necessarily political freedom of any specific kind, just simple, human freedom. Freedom from the Organisations which are already sharpening their claws, ready to catch them for life; freedom from Eternal Discipline; freedom from the Rat-Race; freedom from the oppression of the Old Ones. Japan is even more of a gerontocracy than most societies. Old men assume that there is special merit in age – which is a general fallacy; the reaction of much-tried youth is the belief that there is special merit in youth – which is equally mistaken.

It is the riot-police who personify the defenders of the hated bastions of power so the rebels put on their helmets and fight the riot police. They don't fight for the security of jobs; for better conditions; for a materially more hopeful future: they fight *against* these. They will have the best jobs for the asking, anyway. Once they step on the escalator, they will rise and rise fast and automatically, to great heights, so long as they conform. But they revolt precisely against the grey, eventless, rigid, conformist life which is in store for them on the escalator. They also know that no great exertions are required from them at the university. They will never fail: their failure, as I have pointed out, would be the failure of the selectors and that would never do. But they *want* to fail or, at least, to be able to fail; they want to be tested; they want to prove themselves. They want responsibility – the bogey of modern Japanese society – because without responsibility a man can achieve nothing; without responsibility a man remains a cipher. They refuse to remain just members of honoured and respected groups: they want to be individuals. Student revolts – in Japan as anywhere else – are complex social affairs which will engage the attention of devoted scientists for a long time. But the revolt in Japan – much more than anywhere else – is the revolt of the Individual. In other countries the Individual may aspire to more rights, to social justice, to a saner and more human society; in Japan he aspires to be born.

I heard a distinguished dean of a faculty ask one of his rebellious students (the conversation was exquisitely polite), what the students' aim was.

'Our aim? We want to bust society. That's all.'

'And what do you intend to put in its place?'

'Nothing.'

It is this attitude Japanese society fails to grasp. The few who grasp it condemn it as wicked but it is no more wicked than a cry of despair. Society argues with this small minority on the level of right-wing and left-wing politics, trying to refute the doctrines of Mao, Lenin or Castro which, although in the foreground, have little to do with the real issues. Or they promise overdue university reforms, failing to realise that the students' eyes are, in fact, on post-university life.

It is legitimate to ask: on what level can they solve anything? Even if they understood, would their understanding help? You cannot end the Vietnam war; neither can you argue with despair, with a desire for wanton destruction, with a man who cries out in a nightmare.

Understanding always helps. But it is the students themselves, not their elders, who will solve their problems, and
not, I am afraid, in a grand or heroic manner. Problems,
more often than not, tend to sort themselves out. A lot of
students talk of 'permanent revolution' – a phrase Chair-
man Mao publicised after taking it over, like most of his
ideas, from his much greater predecessor, Karl Marx. But
there is no such thing as permanent revolution. As soon as
revolution becomes permanent it ceases to be revolution
and becomes the established order, itself a *target* for revolution. The old revolution has spent itself. The student
revolution will also spend itself: the youthful revolutionaries will soon enough cease to be not only revolutionaries
but also youthful.

Most of them will settle down and become pillars of the
very society they seem to be so keen on destroying. Theirs
will not be the first revolution to be betrayed by its para-
gons. Napoleon was not born an Emperor; the Soviet Union
of Lenin and Trotsky was not a bureaucratic, nationalistic
tyranny of petty officials; the church bequeathed by Christ
to humanity was to be the church of poor, humble and
progressive men. The conflict between freedom and over-
organisation, the clash between growing comfort for all and
less exquisite, artistic beauty for the few, the parallel
growth of prosperity and ugliness is not the problem of
the students only; it is the problem of all of us and not a
simple one in which black and white can easily be told
apart. Their revolution will neither be defeated nor
triumph: it will fade away only to break out in other
forms, in other fields, under different flags and slogans, led
by new protesters. And to add insult to injury, some of the
vast companies are already fishing in the troubled university waters, keen on recruiting the most militant student
leaders. These young heroes, they say, show initiative; and
initiative is the stuff good businessmen are made of.

Driving

The steering-wheel of a motor-car has the same effect on a modern, civilised man as the smell of blood has on the average tiger.

But the Japanese is no average tiger. He is a suppressed, frustrated and over-teased tiger, forced by sadistic tiger-tamers to keep smiling and blowing when he feels like growling and devouring the boss. Sitting behind the steering wheel he does not feel malicious; he is not after blood: he simply throws all restrictions and discipline to the wind. He is not out to harm others; his aim is to cure himself; to get rid of his worries, humiliating memories, suppressions. While he drives he is free and anonymous: as soon as he stops, he becomes once again a meek, conforming member of society.

Outwardly, all Japanese cars are models of tidiness and cleanliness. I did not see one single dirty – or even not-spotlessly-clean – car during my last visit in Japan. A clean car is part of one's appearance, a sign of self-respect and respect for others, like spotless clothing. A car must stop occasionally, and then everyone can see it, so it must be clean. But so long as it is moving, it is one of many cars in busy traffic, it is anonymous. It is not a means of communication; not even a status symbol; it is a cure for taut and tattered nerves.

Compared with Japanese drivers, the French are meek, over-cautious and patient, the Italians restrained and hyper-courteous. Siam is the only place which belongs to the same school of driving. As an official at the British Embassy in Bangkok (it could easily have been Tokyo) said to me: 'Back in England, on my first day of leave, I performed a perfectly decent – nay, courteous – piéce of East-Asian driving. I was fined ten guineas with three guineas costs and my licence was endorsed.'

Rush-hour traffic in Tokyo has to be seen to be believed. What they do not do in the way of cutting in, crazy corner-ing, acrobatic overtaking and unindicated, or even mislead-ing, changes of direction is not worth doing. With this type of driving one would not survive five minutes even in Rome, simply because no one would be expecting such feats: but in Tokyo every driver is *expected* to perform the physically impossible; every driver is *expected* to drive like a criminal lunatic let out on parole. The only sensible thing they do (or so it seems to a visitor from Britain) is to drive on the left – although that, too, depends on the mood of the moment. You would think they never touch their indicators but they do, quite often. A flickering left indicator means: I am slowing down. Or: I am accelerating. Or: I'm turning left. Or: I am turning right. Or: I forgot to switch it off. Or: you would be ill-advised to pay any attention to indicators.

It is an old joke – I heard it many times on my first visit to Tokyo – that the former suicide-torpedo pilots had be-come taxi-drivers but were longing to get their old jobs back because they were so much less dangerous.

Or it used to be a joke; it is stark reality today.

I heard about a not infrequent type of accident in Japan. Two people meet in the street, have a chat and are about to part. On taking leave, they start bowing and in their zeal for courtesy they keep shuffling backwards and – still bowing – step off the pavement. As soon as they touch the road, a car whizzes by, runs them over and kills them.

Both victim and killer are true symbols of Japan. The little man walking with deep ceremonious bows into his grave; and the maniacal motorist who does not wish to kill the man but certainly wants to kill the ceremonious bow.

A word or two on taxis. They are – need I say? – the worst offenders, the most respected and feared among all vehicles. I often noticed taxi-drivers forging ahead in the murderous traffic like demons out of hell, although they were timid and trembling, dreading every turn of the wheel. They *cannot* drive cautiously: there is an *esprit de corps*. People, including other taxi-drivers, expect all taxi-drivers to drive like werewolves – if that be an apt simile – so like werewolves they drive.

Japanese taxis differ from others in some remarkable features:

(1) Drivers do not expect and in most cases do not even accept tips. They are too proud.

(2) Taxis are very cheap – perhaps the only cheap commodity in Japan.

(3) You cannot open the door of a taxi in Japan from the outside: only the driver can open it for you from his seat, by pushing a button. In other words: you cannot get into a taxi unless the driver lets you in. If he approves of you he will open the door; if he doesn't he won't. If he disapproves of you violently he will open the door suddenly, just to hit you in the belly, close it again and drive off with a happy laugh.

(4) There are some periods of the day (after lunch and at about 10.30 or 11 p.m. which is the surprisingly early closing time for the Ginza) when it is impossible to get a taxi. Even if you see an empty cab it will not stop; if it

stops at a light or in traffic you can't get in (see previous paragraph). The only way to get a taxi at these times without considerable delay is to wave a 1,000-yen note (£1.20p or $2.75) as you stand on the pavement, indicating that you are prepared to give the driver that sum irrespective of the length of the journey. Then taxis will suddenly queue up for you. Japanese taxi-drivers refuse a shilling tip; but they don't mind being overpaid eight or ninefold. Pride has its limits. (If I had their income, my pride would have its limits too; it has, as it is.)

(5) In Israel, if a taxi stops for a moment, the driver grabs a newspaper or a book and starts reading; the Japanese taxi-man grabs a piece of paper stuck on cardboard, takes out his pen and starts scribbling furiously. They all seem to be graphomaniacs, they keep writing and leave Lope de Vega, with his many hundreds of comedies and tragedies, and his thousands of poems and tales, at the post.

In London I go almost everywhere by car. I have always felt slightly guilty about it: I was driving almost as much as a professional. Japanese taxi-drivers have put my conscience at ease and redressed the balance: I drive more than they but they write more than I.

Manners

A quarter of an hour in Japan will convince you that you are among exquisitely well-mannered people. People who live on a hopelessly overcrowded island have to respect one another's privacy – or rather, would have to if they had any privacy. But they don't. So courtesy has a double function: it is courtesy and it is substitute privacy. Take, for example, the little red telephones in the streets, shops, halls of hotels. The instrument is situated on a table, or on a counter – they have no space to spare for booths. You conduct your most confidential business transactions, your intimate love-quarrels in public; yet in perfect privacy. Anybody, any passer-by, could listen-in, but nobody does. A man's telephone-receiver is his castle.

You will, of course, immediately notice their mania for bowing. Everybody keeps bowing to everybody else, with the ceremonious solemnity of a courtier yet with a great deal of natural and inimitable grace. Bowing is neither less nor more silly than shaking hands or kissing the cheek, but it is quainter, more formal, more oriental; it is also infectious. After a few hours you start bowing yourself. But you bow too deeply or not deeply enough; you bow to the wrong man at the wrong time; you do not clasp your hands in front of you which is bad; or you do which is worse. You'll discover that the Japanese have a complicated

hierarchy in bowing: who bows to whom, how deeply and for how long. One of the American states had an early traffic law which laid down that if two cars met at an intersection, neither was to move before the other had gone. Similarly, if two Japanese bow, neither is to straighten up before the other stands erect in front of him. A little complicated to us; they manage it without difficulty and even the smallest difference in rank, standing, age, social position will be subtly reflected in that split second one man's bow is shorter than the other's. In many cases there are clear-cut differences in position and no difficulties. The basic rules inside the family: 'The wife bows to her husband, the child bows to his father, younger brothers to elder brothers, the sister bows to all brothers of whatever age.'* I saw babies carried in Japanese style on their mothers' backs in clever little saddles, and whenever mother bowed, baby bowed too, somewhat condescendingly, from his majestic height. Japanese stores employ bowing girls who stand at the top of escalators and whose only duty is to bow deeply and deferentially to all and sundry (the Japanese equivalent of our page-boys who turn revolving doors for us). On the famous and fast Tokaido Line between Tokyo and Osaka two conductors enter the carriage in a slightly theatrical scene. They march to the middle of the coach, bow ceremoniously in both directions and then start checking the tickets. In one of the parks of Nara I met a deer. I bought a pack of food for him. He came up to me, looked into my eyes and bowed deeply. It was no chance gesture: it was a proper and courteous bow. Perhaps deer are more imitative than I knew; perhaps if they see people bowing all the time they get into the habit too; perhaps it is something genetic and is in the blood

* Ruth Benedict: *The Chrysanthemum and the Sword*, Secker and Warburg.

of Japanese deer. I do not know; but I do know that the deer bowed to me, then jumped at me and snatched the little food-bag from my hand.

In this, too, the deer was a true Japanese. You can often see people bowing to each other with ceremonious serenity at bus-stops. As soon as the bus arrives, the bowing gentlemen are transformed into savages, they push each other aside, tread on each other's toes and shove their elbows into each other's stomachs.

You will also notice that many people carry beautifully wrapped parcels. These are gifts, another charming Japanese courtesy amounting to a mania. They bring gifts on every possible occasion, almost matching our own frenzy at Christmas-time. Not that in addition to the permanent gift-seasons they do not have their special seasons. They have, in fact, three such seasons: New Year, mid-year and end of the year. At least we call gifts *gifts*; in Japan they have a different name for each occasion (*otoshi-dama* for the New Year, *chugen* for the mid-year and *seibo* for the end of the year gift). At least we can *send* our gifts; the poor Japanese has to call on the recipient and hand them over personally, bowing deeply.

The rules about wrapping-paper seem a trifle intricate at first sight but this is not really so. For the foreigner it is enough to know that *hosho, noriire, hanshi* and *noshigami* are considered the best papers, and that for certain lesser occasions *danshi, torinoko, sugiwaragami* and *nishinoushi* are less pretentious and so more appropriate. Once this is remembered the *gaijin* does not need to bother about details. But that much he must memorise, otherwise – well, I do not wish to sound insulting but such things *have* happened – he may wrap something in *nishinoushi* instead of *noshigami*.

The *method* of wrapping is, of course, of decisive importance. 'Wrinkling must be avoided and the folding must be precise. Ordinarily the paper is wrapped so that the last fold comes up on top of the package at the right-hand edge with the end of the paper extending all the way to the left-hand edge of the package. One must be careful about the way this paper is folded, for people are sensitive about it, and it would be rude indeed to send a gift folded as for an unhappy occasion on an ordinary or happy occasion.' Reasonable enough; no one likes to be congratulated on his death.

However, if you send fish, fowl, some other foodstuff or animals (birds, dogs or race-horses) you do not need to wrap them up. You arrange the gifts 'on leaves of Mongolia oak, Japanese cypress, Japanese cedar, pine or nandina', and place them on a tray or basket.

You must be extremely careful with this kind of gift. Once I committed the *faux-pas* of sending a lady a race-horse on Korean cypress instead of Japanese cypress. I was never received by her again.

'Gifts with a red-and-white cord should be tied so that the red cord is on the right; and when using gold-and-silver cord, the gold should be on the right.' But as time marches on, fewer and fewer people commit *harakiri* on realising that they used the gold-and-silver cord with the gold on the left.

This information comes from *Japanese Etiquette*, by the World Fellowship Committee of the YWCA, Tokyo,* an indispensable little book, full of useful hints about such things as how to bow when sitting on the floor. ('One places the hands on the floor, palms down, four or six inches apart and bows between the hands, bringing the head to within four or six inches of the floor.') It also teaches you that when leaving a Japanese house in which you are staying

* Published by C. E. Tuttle.

you always have to declare 'Itte mairimasu' (I am going now), and on returning 'Tadaima' (I am just back). To say on arrival that you are just leaving or on leaving that you have just come back is seen as trifling with your hostess's feelings.

There is, of course, another way. Just treat everyone as your normal instincts prompt. Do not regard anyone as quaint and exotic – remember that you are quainter and more exotic yourself. Approach everybody with kindness and the respect due to every other person, and never mind on which side the gold in that gold-and-silver cord ends up. All will be perfectly all right. (If you feel that you *must* bow sitting on the floor, as I certainly did – practise it when alone.)

The exquisite manners of the Japanese can be exasperating. First of all, they slow everything down. In principle I have the highest admiration for a man who refuses to hurry. Our dependence on the clock is regrettable and the notion that 'time is money' is repulsive; time is much more precious than money, so it ought to be squandered. Nevertheless, whether we like it or not, we Westerners are the children of a rushing and scrambling urban civilisation and we are, at times, slightly irritated by the Japanese habit of beating about the bush and avoiding the point with the utmost care. More and more Japanese accept Western ways and are resigned to raising the point when it seems to be inevitable. But do not hurry them; this is one of the things you have to accept as one accepts the weather. It is elementary politeness to waste other people's time as well as your own.

The air-conditioning in our hotel room went wrong every day, so that the room was either unbearably hot or was suddenly turned into a refrigerator, nay a deep freeze. Every day we asked the clerk at the front desk to have it repaired. Every other day our request was noted with exquisite courtesy, then ignored. But every other-other day a little man appeared with portable steps and a torch. He came in, bowed deeply and smiled. Then he ascended the steps, switched on his torch and flashed it around the grille. He came down, smiled, bowed, picked up his steps and departed.

Next day I would go to the front desk, smile, bow and complain again, telling them that we were melting or freezing. This complaint stigmatized me as a boorish and hopelessly ill-mannered *gaijin*. Had not the man *been*? It was quite immaterial – from the point of view of a higher, oriental philosophy – whether he had mended the air-conditioning or not. His appearance clearly proved that my first complaint had been accepted, looked into, treated with respect – so what more did I want?

The Art of Saying No is not one of the great Japanese arts. I shall never learn it myself and in this respect I am closely akin to the Japanese. To say a plain 'yes' or 'no' is not the best of manners in Britain either: it is much nicer to be vague and incoherent, not to *know* anything, not to be too decisive. In Japan *no* is definitely a rude word, to be avoided or, in the case of utmost emergency, paraphrased.

More often than not they simply use *yes* for *no*. Well, it is one way of solving the problem. 'Did you mean this?' you ask someone who meant the exact opposite. 'Yes,' he will reply politely. 'Or did you mean that?' The answer again is: 'Yes.' 'Do I have two heads?' 'Yes.' 'Or three?' 'Yes.' World Wars have started because of smaller mis-understandings.

If you ask a Japanese a question he does not understand, he will smile politely, because pointing out that he has failed to understand might imply that you expressed yourself obscurely; if you ask him a question which he understands perfectly but which happens to be embarrassing, he will also smile politely. In other words, if he doesn't understand you he will act as if he did; if he does understand you he will act as if he didn't.

Every instruction is accepted with a polite bow and a *yes*. 'If Mr Soandso calls please tell him to go without delay to the Office of Weights and Measures.' Bow, 'yes.' 'Please send this letter by special messenger to the Guatemalan Embassy.' Nod and *'yes.'* Whether the person addressed understood you or not remains a secret. For a time, at any rate.

A further confusion is possible based on linguistic differences: not a matter of misunderstanding the actual words, but of wording the same ideas differently. Never ask a Japanese a negative question. If you ask him: 'Aren't you bored stiff with me?' he or she – the most courteous person on the earth – will answer with a firm and unhesitating *yes*. Meaning *no*. His *yes* does not mean at all that he *is* bored, or that he is prepared to admit it. It only means that he always agrees with your question as if to say: 'Yes – I am not.'

(Many Europeans are misled by the English habit of negative questions. The question: 'You don't mind coming for a walk?' gets the ready reply: 'Yes.' Not meaning that he minds coming but yes, he will come with pleasure.)

Even the young are well-mannered in Japan which is saying a lot. Revolutionary student leaders conform by being ill-mannered when the occasion requires it; but in private they will be as courteous as anyone else. Sometimes too polite for my liking. I found myself more than once in the company of young students, all under twenty-five and some of them notorious agitators. They were always embarrassingly polite to me. I suddenly grasped the sad truth: this reverence was due to my age. 'Good gracious,' I thought, 'they venerate me.'

'Yes, they are courteous enough but their politeness is only skin deep.'

This is a comment resident Europeans and Americans keep whispering into your ear. The remark is untrue on different levels.

Japanese courtesy is an ancient tradition. Francis Xavier, the Christian missionary, one of the first Westerners to reach Japan, wrote home in the middle of the sixteenth century: 'They are people of very good manners, good in general, and not malicious; they are men of honour to a marvel, and prize honour above all else in the world.'*

So Japanese courtesy has a long tradition. Nor is it 'skin-deep' in the sense that it is purely formal and they do not really care. They often go out of their way to be helpful. This is obvious from brief encounters in the street (they run after you to redirect you, having noticed that you took the wrong turning) as well as on more complicated levels.

Sometimes it is explained by the whispering foreign residents that what they mean is something more elaborate. The Japanese are, at heart, temperamental, even violent people and they – much more than other peoples – have to *force* themselves to be courteous, indeed overcourteous, otherwise they would behave like savages.

This is a strange argument. Forced self-discipline is the very meaning of courtesy and of civilisation. We are all savages underneath; civilisation is a veneer (see the history of the present century); civilisation teaches us not to behave as we are naturally inclined: not to grab, not to push, not to shout, not to kill – but to bow and hiss and smile. Skin-deep courtesy is a lot of courtesy, particularly if you re-

---

* Translated by C. R. Boxer and quoted by Richard Storry, *op. cit.*

member how thick some people's skin is. And skin-deep courtesy is infinitely better than the thick, undisguised, robust rudeness you meet in many other countries. The gist of the whispered criticism is simply: Japanese courtesy is useless because they would be terribly rude if only they were not so polite.

Soup and Haggis

Just two more brief notes on Japanese manners.

(1) Eating soup has more dangers than almost anything else. When eating soup you must make a fearful noise. It is a sign of appreciation. If you don't, your hostess will think: 'What an ill-mannered lout.' But if you *do*, she will think: 'No reasonably well brought-up *European* makes such disgusting noises when eating soup. He must be an ill-mannered lout.'

(2) It has happened only once that I felt very strongly, almost passionately, that politeness was overdone. A Japanese industrialist once told me that he had been in Scotland and loved it. I nodded and agreed that Scotland was a lovely country.

'I love haggis,' he added.

'That's overdoing it a bit,' I thought, but said nothing.

'I grew very fond of haggis,' he went on.

I kept quiet but my soul frowned.

'Very, very fond.'

'I am not a Scotsman,' I said at last, softly. I meant to convey that I appreciated his effort to be flattering about haggis but there is a limit to everything. And by stating that I wasn't a Scotsman I was hinting that he should enthuse about steak and kidney pie instead. Or goulash. But he went on: 'I miss haggis. I miss it very much.' And, after a short pause, romantically: 'I miss it all the time.'

Then the incredible truth dawned on me. He was not being polite: he was speaking the unvarnished truth. Here he was, a Japanese gentleman of fifty-three, a manufacturer of men's underwear, rich in material goods, yet a little unhappy because he could not get a haggis in Yokohama.

Beauty and Ugliness

When I was in Japan, the Japanese were gravely insulted. They had been called by one of their compatriots the ugliest people in the world.

'The Japanese,' wrote Mr Ichiro Kawasaki, 'are perhaps physically the least attractive people with the exception of the Pygmies and Hottentots. Members of the so-called Mongolian race to which the Japanese belong have flat, expressionless faces, high cheek-bones, and oblique eyes. Their figures are also far from being shapely with a disproportionately large head, an elongated trunk, and short, often bowed legs.'*

I don't know how beautiful or otherwise Hottentots are. I cannot recall ever having seen one. Perhaps they do not even exist, but were just invented for the sake of disparaging comparisons. Smollett, about two hundred years ago, was already complaining (about the Italians, not the Japanese) that their 'inns are enough to turn the stomach of a muleteer' and that 'the victuals . . . were cooked in such a manner as to fill a Hottentot with loathing.'

Whether Hottentots exist or not, it is clear from the context that Mr Kawasaki meant nothing complimentary. He was Japanese Ambassador to Argentina when his book

* *Japan Unmasked*, C. E. Tuttle.

appeared (first in English) and created what more common persons than I would call a stink. He was recalled, put in cold storage and informed that he would soon be retired. The Foreign Ministry hotly denied that this decision had anything to do with his book. He had stayed long enough in Argentina, it was stated, and was approaching retiring age. If an ambassador is a gentleman sent abroad to lie in the interest of his country, then a Foreign Ministry is a collection of gentlemen staying at home, doing the same. Kawasaki spent less than a year in Argentina and even in Japan people are retired when they *reach* and not when they *approach* retiring age. Perhaps Kawasaki was retired, after all, because he saw less beauty in the Japanese than the present Foreign Minister; perhaps, because he had failed to obtain permission for publishing his book, as was his duty. There was quite a hullabaloo about the book and I always thought this question of permission was the crux of the matter. But no one ever put the question to Kawasaki. So I asked him. He told me: no, he had not asked permission because he had regarded this new book as a revised version of an older one, called *The Japanese Are Like That*. But in his own preface to *Japan Unmasked* he calls his work 'a completely new book'. (Is this a literary or a diplomatic blunder?)

Be that as it may, Mr Kawasaki, instead of being angry with the Foreign Ministry, should feel undying gratitude to it. 'I am not a distinguished diplomat; I am an *ex*-tinguished diplomat,' he protested at a luncheon, and his extinction, his recall, turned his book into a *succès de scandale*. He was inundated with offers to unmask many things: Japanese sex-life, politics, big business; he was requested to unmask Korea, Taiwan, the United Nations and the United States; he was requested to unmask diplomatic life and the latest offer was to unmask the moon. If he accepts only half of these offers he will become the greatest professional unmasker of the century.

It is often said that the Japanese are very sensitive; they hate all criticism, however mild, and refuse to read or listen to anything unfavourable about themselves. I have found them much more reasonable in this respect, carrying fewer chips on their shoulders, than their neighbours, the Australians, and I am pleased to report that their masochistic instincts are as highly and healthily developed as those of most nations. When I was in Tokyo, Kawasaki's book was published in Japanese and sold like hot cakes.

Is Kawasaki right or wrong about the ugliness of the Japanese? True, the Japanese are small in stature but so are the Italians, usually referred to as extremely good-looking people. They are growing, however: both Italians and Japanese. They are much better off than before and shortness of stature is closely connected with poverty and malnutrition.

It is also true, I think, that the legs of the Japanese are shorter than they ought to be because of their habit of squatting, or more precisely of sitting, on their heels. This posture – practised for long centuries – hinders the proper development of the legs. Now, however, with the influx of modern and revolutionary ideas, the Japanese are beginning to understand that the function of legs is to be stood on, not sat on, so this defect may slowly be remedied. And anyway the Japanese often wear *kimonos* (unlike Italians who never do) and *kimonos* have outstanding advantages; (a) they look distinguished and beautiful and (b) they cover up everything – girth, legs, stomachs, behinds.

So if you insist on long legs Mr Kawasaki's statements contain a grain of truth. But no more. The Japanese are certainly not ugly. I admit that I spent only brief moments contemplating male beauty in Japan. Male beauty leaves me cold whether I am in Sweden, in Japan or in the land of the Hottentots. But I watched Japanese women almost incessantly with what are – or at least used to be – expert eyes. I am now approaching the Age of Consent,* but I was always aware that I was in a land of very beautiful women, whether they wore their *kimonos* or not.

In Japan you are surrounded by beauty. The Japanese create beauty everywhere. (In Tokyo one occasionally has the feeling that their talent for creating ugliness equals their talent for creating beauty, but that is a local problem, of which more later.)

First, it is their tidiness and cleanliness you notice. These are virtues I do not respect, or if I may be a shade more explicit, which as a rule I detest. They are the virtues of fat, dull, bourgeois housewives, the virtues of door-polishers, the virtues which make their possessors smug and vulgar. What's more, and worse; tidiness and cleanliness are not only habits, they are a philosophy, a desperate attempt to put everything in its proper place, into a pigeonhole. Everything must belong *somewhere*. Excessive tidiness – tidiness as a religion, not just ordinary and, alas, unavoidable tidiness – is an attempt to create a system where there is no system. Tidiness is over-simplification. Tidiness is the desire to tame *things* – but things are wicked and unmanageable, with a will of their own, much more untameable than meek lions who hop up on to high stools and leap through hoops. Tidiness is tyranny. It is Goethe's effort to fit everything into *Gestalt* (form) or *Gesetz* (law). God, you will notice, is often far from tidy (but the *hausfrau* and her philosopher counterpart, in their infinite goodness, are prepared to forgive God).

And as for cleanliness, it is downright unhealthy and rather dangerous. It is unhygienic. Americans, who live amidst too much hygiene, lose their resistance so that the

---

* This is a legal expression, meaning the age when women consent to one.

tiniest amount of dirt knocks them out and makes them sick. I am for untidiness; and for a modicum of dirt.

But Japan – one of the tidiest and surely *the* cleanest country in the world – can plead extenuating circumstances. Japan is an overcrowded island and the Japanese have no room for untidiness. In a Japanese home every square inch is cleverly utilised and everything must be put in its proper place because there is no other place for it. When you get into a commuter's train, you see the briefcases neatly stacked on the rack, one briefcase closely pressed against the next, all standing with their handles upwards, like books on a shelf, so as to occupy the absolute minimum space although half of the rack may be empty.

Tidiness in Japan can be forgiven, or at least understood. But I did find their cleanliness a bit disconcerting. Everyone is always neatly dressed. The men's white shirts are invariably impeccable – they give you the impression that no shirt is worn longer than an hour. Many people wear white gloves: taxi-drivers, bus-conductors, even gardeners and dustmen. And when I say white I mean white. How gardeners and dustmen can keep their white gloves spotless, is beyond me. Cars – as I have mentioned – are always impeccable, their chromium gleaming. You sit down in a café or a restaurant and the first thing you will automatically be offered is a hot face towel: you wipe your face and hands and feel refreshed. Everything is not only clean but also new in Japan – at least in the inner districts of the larger towns; tables, chairs, seat-covers, vases, ashtrays, cushions. As soon as anything begins to fade or is slightly damaged, it is thrown away. Japan is, you often feel, an improved version of the United States.

Homes, of course, are spotless too. As people do not wear shoes inside their houses, it is easier to keep a house clean in Japan than elsewhere where dust, snow and slush are carried inside.

Hired Japanese cleaners are thorough and conscientious: sweeping dirt under the carpet is not one of their national traits. But here, as everywhere, there are limits. A European ambassador told me that the man who cleaned his study at the embassy was a treasure, a trusted and much loved old employee, and, although a male, a paragon of all charwomanly virtues. But he refused to clean the floor. Everything else, yes; the floor, no. 'He seems to think,' his employer explained to me, 'that if the *gaijin* is so stupid as to wear shoes inside his house, then he obviously does not *want* to have his floor clean.'

It is often said that the Japanese are extremely clean at home, or inside any house or office, but dirty and untidy outside. 'Go and look at a railway station,' I was told, 'and you'll be horrified.' I went and *was* horrified; horrified by the cleanliness of the place. Although already shining white, it was being cleaned, washed, brushed and scrubbed all the time. The floor was cleaner than many a restaurant table I have come across in Europe.

The one great redeeming feature of this disheartening cleanliness and tidiness is that it is always accompanied by a sense of beauty. The Japanese have a strong aesthetic sense: they beautify, embellish, adorn and decorate everything they touch. A sandwich in Japan is not just a sandwich, it is a work of art. It is cut into an artistic shape – it can be circular, octagonal or star-shaped – and given a colour scheme with carefully placed bits of tomato, coleslaw and pickles. There is, as a rule, a flag or some other decoration hoisted on top. Every dish is aimed at the eye as well as the palate. Every tiny parcel, from the humblest little shop, radiates some original charm or at least tries to, and reflects pride: look how well done it is! Every taxi-driver has a small vase in front of him, with a beautiful, fresh, dark-red or snow-white flower in it. Once I watched a man at the counter in a fish-restaurant. *Sushi* and *sashimi*

– the famous raw fish of Japan – comes in many forms and cuts, and it takes about ten years for a man to reach the counters of a first-class establishment. The man I watched was not bored with his somewhat monotonous job : he enjoyed every minute of it to the full, took immense pride in it. Michaelangelo could not have set a freshly carved Madonna before you with more pride and satisfaction than this cook felt when he put a freshly carved piece of raw fish on your plate.

The Japanese are unable to touch anything without beautifying it, shaping it into something pretty and pleasing to the eye. One evening I was walking in one of the slummy suburbs of Tokyo and saw a heap of rubbish outside the backyard of a factory. It was an immense mountain of rubbish, but it was not just thrown out as it came; all the boxes were piled into a graceful if somewhat whimsical pyramid, while the loose rubbish was placed on top as artistic and picturesque decoration. Someone must have spent considerable time in converting that heap of rubbish almost into a thing of beauty.

This universal striving for beauty explains a great deal. I have said that psychoanalysis is gaining ground in Japan, but only slowly. Even so, it spreads more rapidly than neuroses. The Japanese take pride in their work; they *create* – no matter what, but they create all the time. They participate. Nothing is accepted just as it comes; nothing is thrown at you. The phrase, 'I couldn't care less' does not exist in Japanese; they couldn't care more. Every charwoman arrives early, leaves late and takes pride in the beauty and comfort of the home she has to look after. If there is something special afoot she will turn up on days when she is not supposed to come and you have to think out polite and tricky ways of compensating her because she will flatly refuse extra money and will be deeply hurt by your offer.

A sandwich, then, is not just a sandwich: it is a means of self-expression. A rubbish-heap is not just a rubbish-heap: it is a modernistic, abstract sculpture which could be called 'The Poetry of Urban Waste'. Tokyo is not only the largest city in the world; not only the ugliest but also one of the most beautiful. The eruptive sense of beauty of its people is overwhelming. Even in that huge conglomeration of men and concrete this ubiquitous sense of beauty keeps a man a man, makes every occupation – even the dullest – a job worth doing because it can be done a little better. This sense of beauty makes life a satisfying experience, not just a piece of drudgery performed by dreary robots. It turns every dustman into an artist; makes every Japanese a creator. And that leaves little time for neurosis.

Snobbery Japanese Style

Western-style snobbery is a tender flower in Japan, a new growth. Like all things occidental it reached Japan only late. They had to start from scratch. But here again they proved excellent pupils and are doing remarkably well.

The Snobbery Miracle is almost as glorious as the Economic Miracle, but it is not too subtle as yet. It has a mid-nineteen-fiftyish aura about it and, all things considered, it resembles the crude American form rather than the slightly more sophisticated British variety.

When put into its proper historical and sociological perspective, the achievement of the Japanese snob is remarkable. He has had an incredibly hard time. It was less than a hundred years ago that the last *samurai* uprising was defeated. The *samurai* as a ruling class had been abolished. Half of the members of this class fled headlong into commerce and industry, the rest lingered on, living in the past. Their morality and their influence, however, survived their loss of power. Theirs used to be a world in which the sword was the only noble tool under the sun and anything to do with trade was beneath contempt. The true *samurai* refused to learn arithmetic because it smelled of commerce; he was proud of his ignorance and stupidity, like so many ruling classes all over the world. Saigo, the leader of their revolt and a splendid character, was beheaded on the battlefield at his own request, but his (and his dog's) statue still stands in Tokyo. The introduction of conscription was the last blow which, with its implication that a peasant could become a soldier and could fight just like a member of the ancient warrior class, triggered off the revolution. Perhaps the idea that the peasant, too, could die, could be shot to smithereens was acceptable; but the idea that he could *wear a sword* was intolerable.

This was the *samurai's* attitude towards the peasant. Merchants belonged to a still lower class, below the peasant. The thought that this class, the lowest of the low, could rise one day to a leading position higher than the peasant, higher than the *samurai* – seemed ridiculous. That they should one day brandish Japan's new sword – the economic weapon – meant turning all values upside down.

But the Japanese learn fast. Whenever floods threaten their homes they do not flee: they dive headlong into the menacing tide and learn, first of all, how to swim.

There is no namedropping in Japan *à l'anglaise*. The Japanese does not want to be proud of his friends or connections: he wants to be proud of himself. There is little outright ostentation in the classic *nouveau riche* manner. There is no aristocratic snobbery (titles have been abolished; a high-born fool is just an ordinary fool). It is not even his money the Japanese wants to show off. Even the most influential tycoon will have no great personal fortune in the American sense of the word. He will have all the trimmings, the house, the car, the chauffeur, trips abroad in the grand manner, high life in ruinously expensive restaurants and night clubs, but not much money of his own. What the Japanese wants to show off is his status, his position, his power.

Japanese snobbery has three main outlets.

(1) In the pre-history of the new-style snobbery (i.e.

about ten years ago, at the start of the boom) everything moved on a rather primitive level, just as it did in post-war lower-middle-class Britain when a television aerial was a coveted status symbol. In Japan people talked of the three C's: Car, Cooler and Colour. *Car* meant car; *cooler* meant air-conditioning; *colour* meant colour-television. In other words they were after what sober economists call durable goods, intoxicating possessions of this Age of Technology. All these dreams were soon universally realised, and – still during this period – the Three Old C's had to be replaced by Three New C's: Cottage, Central Heating and Concubine.

Cottage means a hut or a palace in the country – a snobbery (or need?) in the Anglo-Saxon world, in Scandinavia (the *stuga*) and even in the Soviet Union (the *dacha*) as well as in Japan. Central Heating, surprisingly, came only after air-conditioning but it arrived soon enough. A Concubine is not a new idea in Japan, but is fairly new as a status symbol. The spiritual basis of Japanese snobbery – of all snobbery – is not the claim that 'I enjoy it' but the battlecry: 'I can afford it.' If a man can afford to be the patron of a really fashionable geisha-girl and can maintain her in a magnificent house and in the grand style, he has really made it. So ageing and decrepit tycoons visit their geishas with astonishing frequency. All they want from them is that, once in bed, the girl should leave them alone and let them read the financial pages of the *Mainichi Shimbun*. Many of them would prefer to sleep at home, in their own beds. But women have always been more snobbish and more ambitious than men and it is their wives who chase the poor fellows out into the dark and insist that they sleep with their expensive geishas. They heave a sigh and off they go.

(2) The Stone Age of Snobbery passed. Serious car-production for the home market started only in 1965

(second-hand trading in cars began seriously only in 1967). In the early days there was the 'My Car' campaign. The slogan, 'My Car' (in English) was hammered home with such ferocity and insistence that the phrase, 'My-Car' became part of the Japanese language. Now everyone – which means almost everyone who will ever achieve it – has his own car. So what's the next step? As the Japanese do not produce huge cars, the black, chauffeur-driven but smaller limousine has to do for most tycoons. A few are driven around in large American automobiles or expensive German or even more expensive British models. Foreign cars are much in demand. They do not have to be good as long as they are expensive.

Cars have an overpowering fascination everywhere for a while, then – as soon as 'everyone can afford a car' – they lose their snob-value. Japanese one-upmanship now reaches out for anything unique. The unique prize possession may be a Rolls-Royce, an electric carving knife or a power-driven potato-peeler of staggering design. As long as you are the only one to possess it in the neighbourhood, it matters little what it is.

But the top achievement is to belong to a club – especially to a golf-club. It is the ultimate glory. Once you are a member of a top golf-club, you have achieved – snobologically speaking – salvation. Top clubs do not only carry tremendous prestige but are also very expensive. It may cost £5,000 – $12,000 – just to join. Consequently it will always be a man's firm who pays for him and everyone knows this. His membership only means: 'Look, I'm important enough to be sent into this club.' Sometimes he becomes a true golf-addict; sometimes he hates the game as much as his geisha-chasing counterpart hates to make love. Indeed, he may be one and the same man, in which case life – with golf and geishas – must be endless suffering for him. But he will do his duty: he will practise, study the game and play golf with the singleminded devotion of all Japanese dedicated to a task. He knows that life has its seamy side.

When an aspiring young man is posted to, say, Rangoon, he will be told: 'Well, it is rather going into exile but we'll let you join the best golf-club there. And if you do really well, then, on your return we may – yes: *may* – let you join one of our own golf-clubs at home.'

Having heard this he would be ready to go not only to Rangoon, but to hell.

If he *is* allowed to join the golf-club on his return, his firm will choose the appropriate club for him, pay his entrance fee and subscription. There are special clubs for junior executives, middle-rank executives, senior executives, managing directors, vice-presidents and presidents – and of course the size of their companies matters, too. In America when a man forges ahead in age, rank and salary, he will change his house and neighbourhood. In Japan this is impossible; in Japan he changes his golf-club.

(3) The latest development is Western snobbery. I am glad to report that Britain – always the darling of snobs all over the world – has lost nothing of her attractiveness. Everything English is coveted and expensive. English textiles are often no better than the latest Japanese products, but so long as they cost twice as much they have nothing to fear. Perfumes and cosmetics must come from France, ladies' dresses must be designed either in France or in Italy. It must be added, however, that the *kimono* holds its position more successfully than many other Japanese traditions. This is less because it is beautiful – as it certainly is – but because it costs much more than a Western dress. A few hundred pounds is nothing out of the way for an evening *kimono* while a Western couturier has to offer something quite extraordinary for that price.

On the whole Japanese snobbery works against traditional values and customs. Everyone is dressed (for work) in Western suits and dresses; the young eat less rice and more potatoes; less fish and more meat. Pizza is competing with raw fish and *sake* is giving ground to whisky (£14 a bottle); cocktail-parties replace geisha-parties. Hamburgers have come to stay and the hot dog reared its ugly head long ago.

You must also have a hobby. No matter what, but a hobby – preferably with a new, Western touch. I taught a group of elderly purveyors of frozen food tiddly-winks (completely unknown before) and gained their everlasting gratitude. You must try to mix as many foreign words in your Japanese as you can muster. And you must eat French bread. Long French bread has a new but fast-spreading snob value; you see more of it than in France. And, of course, cheese. Cheese is a post-war discovery in Japan, the very word did not exist before, and they still call it *cheesu*. If you eat *cheesu* you are somebody; if you really love *cheesu* you have arrived.

I fared pretty well in Japan. My social status was considerable. I have no Rolls-Royce; no electric potato peeler. But God, don't I love *cheesu*.

Ladies and Gentlemen

Man does not live by snobbery alone although sometimes it looks as if he did. Britain's influence does not consist solely of Japanese adoration of Scotch whisky. Indeed, in a few cases British influence can be mistaken for something it isn't. Occasionally a pro-British attitude has nothing to do with liking things British; it is simply one manifestation of a slight anti-American trend. Generally speaking, British English is preferred in Japan; not because it is nicer but because it is not American.

The Japanese character has strong traditional traits but it is also a mosaic. The Japanese went out to learn, to absorb, to imbibe foreign ways, methods, skills. So it is a legitimate question to ask: how British are the Japanese? How American? How Chinese? How French?

How British?

They are very British, of course. Quite a few similarities are obvious and have been dwelt upon many times. Japan is a small, overpopulated island east of Asia; Britain is a small overpopulated island west of Europe. Both are parts of their respective Continents in some ways, very remote from them in many others. Japan's application to join an

104

Asian Common Market could easily have been rejected. Both are the richest and most industrialised nations of their regions. (Japan's position has been confirmed lately while Britain's has become more dubious.) Both peoples reached out far beyond their frontiers to rule other nations and occupy their lands. (While Britain's Empire may be dwindling, Japan's was abolished at the stroke of a pen.) Both people have extremely good manners and worship their ancestors, the British doing it more subtly but no less devoutly than the Japanese.* Both nations have a long, close relationship with the sea and both have got used to thinking in global terms. Both countries are not just monarchies but devoted, almost religious, royalists. When King Farouk of Egypt felt his throne wobbling in 1950, he remarked: 'In half a century from now there will be only five kings left in the world: the kings of Clubs, Diamonds, Hearts and Spades, and the King of England.' But Farouk made a mistake: he forgot the Emperor of Japan. The Emperor of Japan was deprived of his semi-divine status in 1945; the Queen of England has kept hers.

The British and the Japanese character, too, have a great deal in common. Both are reserved and rather shy people, ashamed of their feelings which are always covered up and carefully hidden.

The Japanese ability to create muddle rivals the British. The confusion the Japanese can cause with their refusal to have proper postal addresses is phenomenal. Except in Kyoto and Sapporo (in Hokkaido) they have no street names. They name districts, buildings and intersections (as if in London we had Selfridges and Oxford Circus, but no

---

* 'Ancestor-worship (in Britain) has taken the form of reverence for old houses and churches, the most amazing coinage, the quaintest weights and measures, Guards regiments, public houses, old cars, cricket, above all the hereditary monarchy etc.' *The Rise of the Meritocracy*, by Michael Young, Thames and Hudson.

Oxford Street). They are quite sentimental about this refusal: that is their way, that is their tradition, just as the British were moved to tears when they thought for one horrible moment that they would have to give up Fahrenheit, easily the worst system in the world, invented by an East Prussian. As a result more postmen are in lunatic asylums in Japan than anywhere in the world: nervous breakdown with crying fits is a recognised occupational disease of Japanese postmen. (To speed up its outbreak, Japanese letters are addressed to So-and-so San – *San* meaning Mr, Mrs, *and* Miss.) Somebody told me that when an American exclaimed about this exasperating lack of street names, a Japanese gentleman replied in an amused and somewhat patronising manner: 'Oh you Americans . . . you want a name for *everything*.'

Even Japanese understatement, at least on occasion, rivals the British. Before the war, we had the notorious 'incidents'. An incident – according to the Oxford Dictionary – is a 'subordinate event'. The Manchurian Incident – that subordinate event in Manchuria – changed the history of Japan. Or take the famous surrender broadcast. Japan had been defeated on land, at sea and in the air; the country had been devastated more than Germany by aerial bombardment even *before* the atomic bombs were dropped; then they *were* dropped; and the Soviet Union declared war on Japan. The surrender broadcast summed all this up: 'The war situation has developed not necessarily to Japan's advantage.'

(In a way this understatement was most un-British. *They* always described their own setbacks, defeats and disasters not only with candour but with gusto.)

The relationship between Britain and Japan is a good one. The British Week and Expo both help. These countries want to trade with each other and although British strikes and delays in delivery cause stupefaction in Japan – they simply do not understand this sort of thing – there is no major unsettled issue between the two.

Except the dog crisis. Some British dog-lovers complained that dogs were badly treated in Japan. There was no actual demand to declare war on Japan to liberate oppressed dogs, but considering the fuss dog-lovers can create (second only to the Sunday Observance Society) anything could have happened. I did not quite understand the uproar. I saw that Japanese dogs were kindly treated, well fed, well groomed and rather spoilt. Then I heard that the British complaint was not about Japanese dogs. How the Japanese treated their own dogs was their own internal affair. The outcry was about British dogs exported to Japan: they were British subjects, protected by the Crown and, indeed, the British Embassy was deeply involved in the dog-crisis. A high-ranking diplomat told me that British-Japanese relations were much worse than at the fall of Singapore. Not only were these British dogs insufficiently revered – and that was bad enough – but they were *being bred from too often.* Then, at last, I understood. It was the British puritan speaking: dogs – even dogs sold for breeding – should not copulate too frequently: it is immoral. The puritan's voice was mingled with the voice of the true British humanitarian. Britain, the country where sex-life was practically unknown before 1955, has become the sex-capital of the world. Very well, that has to be accepted with resignation even by dog-lovers. But if human beings are foolish enough to have more sexual intercourse than the greatness of Britain demands, if some of them seek sexual intercourse actually for *pleasure,* that is their own business. It does not mean that poor, innocent animals should be exposed to the same horrors.

How American?

The rest of the world has a stereotyped image, left over
from the twenties, of Americans: the tall businessman
chewing his enormous cigar, hiring and firing people in a
loud, nasal voice, worshipping money and always wearing
a hat when indoors.

But they were very different Americans who arrived in
Japan in 1945. They were modern, tough and efficient young
men; masters of modern techniques and superb administra-
tors. They were led by the Viceroy, a man who loved Japan
but had an imperious and avuncular attitude towards her.
He knew what was best for her and gave orders to act
accordingly.

People invading a country after its unconditional surrender are rarely loved. The Americans always expect love
and never get it; in this single case they expected hatred
and hostility but, for once, they were loved. And respected;
respected as Americans; respected as conquerors.

The Japanese were eager to learn. They wanted to find
out as soon as possible how to be victors and top-dogs.

The world was impressed, the Americans were pleased.
America is the first great power in history which wants to
be loved and loved she was, for the first time since
Columbus.

The Americans then went on to treat the Japanese
generously, and expected gratitude. But if you give cause
to any man – or group – for gratitude he will resent it and
his resentment will produce strong reactions. This time the
Japanese did not prove exceptions to the rule: Japanese
resentment grew in proportion to American nobility of
heart, and by 1952, the end of the occupation, relations
between Americans and Japanese were pretty bad. They
reached their lowest ebb two years later when the Americans exploded a nuclear bomb at Bikini thereby infecting

a number of Japanese fishermen. Understandably, the Japanese were even more sensitive on that point than other nations – and even the others are not exactly fond of nuclear bombs being dropped on their fishermen and the fish they are to eat. The flame of anti-Americanism was fanned by Communists and nationalists, but it died down; and now the relationship between the two countries is very good once again, with only slight, unavoidable undercurrents.

On a superficial level Japan seems to be thoroughly Americanised: the automobiles, the cocktail-parties, the victorious forward march of Bourbon on the rocks, chewing gum and Coca-Cola, hamburgers and cheeseburgers are much in evidence. Japan – as I have mentioned – produces more flavours of ice cream than the United States. The Japanese have also learnt a few less conspicuous but more important things: American business administration, efficiency and technique.

The renewed love affair between the two nations is more sober and critical now than it used to be. It is now a well-tried marriage, they have lived together for quite a while. They have some difficulties over Okinawa and the Security Treaty but even these look like lovers' quarrels. Mr Nixon is anxious to save his friends in power and to remain on good terms with the Japanese, so Okinawa will, most probably, be returned in 1972. In fact, the shoe is on the other foot now: the Americans have quite a few grudges against the Japanese.

They concern business – and business, in the final analysis, is always a more serious matter than mere sovereignty or nuclear bases. First, the Americans complain that the Japanese flood their markets with cheap textiles (to which the Japanese reply that in the year of the bitterest complaint the profits of the American textile industry rose by twenty-one per cent, so it was not doing so desperately badly). The other complaint is that Japan tends to over-protect her currency (one of the strongest in the world, but protected by exchange control regulations as if it were a virgin of sixteen) and, even worse, she overprotects her markets. Japanese motor-cars, for example, sell in huge numbers all over the world but their home market is so heavily protected that foreign cars, although much coveted, are few and far between in the streets of Japan. The Japanese plead that their motor-car industry is new and needs protection. Considering that it is the second largest motor-car industry in the world this pose of the frail flower in need of protection just doesn't wash. The real reasons are that (1) Japan wants to become the *first* motor-car producing country in the world (a far cry) and (2) that her motor-car manufacturers are much happier without foreign competition. The Americans press on hard and with great patience, demanding the liberalisation of Japanese trade policies; the Japanese make concessions when they must but their motor-car industry is not too willing to co-operate. It is – an astounding truth – in the nature of all industries, everywhere, that they prefer larger profits to smaller ones. Any politician, says the industrialist, who gives up sovereignty over this or that part of the country is a wise statesman, fond of intelligent compromise; but the politician who tends to lessen the profit of the industrialist's own particular industry is unpatriotic – well, let's call a spade a spade: a downright traitor.

Admiration for America burns with a brighter flame since the landing on the moon. No one else can do what the Americans did: no one else can be first on the moon again. That prize is gone. But the Japanese staged the first Olympic Games in Asia; they organised the first World Exposition in Asia. I'm sure they are determined that they must be – in due course – the first Asians on the moon.

How Chinese?

Japanese-Chinese relations form two sides of a triangle, America being the third. America is in need of a Far Eastern *protegé*. Mao's China has ceased to act in that capacity and Japan has had to replace it. The United States is responsible for Japan's defence and there are some spots on which great powers are more sensitive than on others. That Japan – the new blue-eyed boy of the Orient – should recognise China, the prodigal son, a really bad hat, is out of the question. But Japan wants to trade with China. What a dilemma! Only Japanese ingenuity could solve it: Japan does not recognise China (she recognises Taiwan) but trades with everyone: China, Taiwan *and* the Soviet Union.

Trade with China is a little less roaring than it once was. The complete disappearance of a Japanese journalist in China strained relations; then the Japanese were taken aback by the peculiar spectacle of the Red Guards Cultural Revolution. And, of course, the Chinese are suspicious of Japan: the crimes of the thirties are not easily forgotten. The Japanese understand the oriental mind better than any of us but they are still puzzled by paranoia. They failed to understand that the so-called Cultural Revolution was a manoeuvre of internal politics. In Holland, and even in Japan, the whole thing would have boiled down to new general elections. Even in Nazi Germany a plebiscite with ninety-nine point eight per cent of votes for the government would have done. But techniques improve and Mao wanted to prove to the world that China could produce a new invention or two. The Cultural Revolution in his eyes was a plebiscite which answered a hundred per cent 'yes'.

But Chinese-Japanese relations go back, of course, a long time before the discovery of America. In the seventh century the Japanese, under Fujiwara Kamatari, were already imitating the T'ang Empire; they took over China's ideo-

111

grams, their ways of life and as much of Chinese culture as they could. The Chinese are very contemptuous about the Japanese: 'They learned everything from us,' they say. The Japanese are equally contemptuous about the Chinese: 'They have learnt nothing since the seventh century.' Mutual contempt has always been a good, reliable basis for friendship, particularly when – as in this case – it covers a great deal of mutual admiration and envy. The Chinese admire Japan's prosperity and advanced industries; while the Japanese throw covetous glances across the sea and are keenly desirous to have the things China has in abundance but which they lack completely: political power and influence.

How French?

A friend of mine ran a small but excellent restaurant near Knightsbridge. One evening a distinguished-looking couple came in and before ordering their meal they enquired where the loo was. The lady was sent behind a small screen at the corner of the restaurant; the gentleman, to his astonishment, was told to follow her. When he returned, he commented: 'If your food is as French as your lavatory, yours must be the best restaurant in London.'

In this respect French influence is even stronger in Japan.

In a Japanese-style restaurant in Tokyo I asked a friend where the Gentlemen's was. He pointed to a little door which I entered. I found two other men standing side by side and engaged in the activity for the sake of which one, as a rule, visits such establishments. Suddenly a door opened and a young, elegant and beautiful lady came out. I was a little taken aback but she was not. Without even looking at the three of us, she washed her hands and walked out quite unconcerned. While I was washing my hands another lady walked in and, paying no attention to the busy men, walked into the cubicle.

'I say,' I reproached my Japanese friend on my return to the table, 'I asked you where the Gentlemen's was.'

'You did,' he nodded, 'and I showed it to you.'

'It wasn't the Gentlemen's. It was the Ladies!'

'Oh that ...' he said with a superior smile, implying: 'how stupid can the *gaijin* get?' – 'Well, it is Ladies' *and* Gentlemen's.'

I presume *San* was written upon the door in Japanese. *San* which – as the reader no doubt remembers – means Mr, Mrs *and* Miss.

The Way They Live

Kanji and Kana

Japanese, unlike many oriental languages (Chinese among them) is not a tonal language You keep hearing stories about a beautiful well-bred lady, trying to speak a tonal language and meaning to say 'Morning dew', but using the wrong tone and saying instead a phrase of the filthiest gutter-language, which even a Chinese drill-sergeant could not utter without blushing.

I was still puzzled by the meaning of 'tone' while investigating the secrets of Japanese. I met a charming young Chinese girl in Tokyo, a Miss Wong, who told me: 'But it's the easiest thing in the world. I'll explain it to you.'

She did. I do not remember all the actual words but the explanation went something like this.

'Let's take the word *wong*, for instance.'

As I could not suggest any other Chinese word, I agreed and said: 'Let's.'

'Now, *wong* pronounced this way – means drum.'

'Yes,' I nodded.

'An ear-drum, too,' she added for the sake of precision.

'Yes. A drum. Or an eardrum.'

'But pronounced this way: *wong*' – and she pronounced it, to my ear, exactly as she did the first *wong* – 'it means butterfly.'

'I see,' I said a little vaguely.

'If you say *wong* – (exactly the same again) – it means:
running up the hill panting. *Wong*, on the other hand,
means autumn harvest. Who would mix that up with
wong, which means to issue meteorological bulletins twice
daily?'

'Who indeed?' I asked, trying to sound ironical at the
expense of such ninnies.

As she stopped there, I said: 'And it's your name, too.'

'My name?' she cried out flabbergasted. 'What has it
got to do with my name? My name is Wong.'

Nothing like this in Japanese. To European ears it is a
normal, pleasant-sounding tongue vaguely resembling
Spanish or Portuguese. A rich language, a difficult language
but not unlearnable.

The serious trouble starts with writing. Japanese
characters are beautiful, picturesque and exotic. And that
is all one can say in their favour. Otherwise theirs is the
most complicated, most cumbersome and most pretentious
script ever invented by man.

It was in the early eighth century that the Japanese felt
in need of an alphabet. Following an ancient Japanese habit
they borrowed it from others. To their misfortune these
'others' were their next-door neighbours, the Chinese.
Chinese writing is based on a childishly simple principle,
well suited to the needs of the stone age: every word is
represented by a special ideograph. Antiquity produced two
important ingenious inventions which changed the fate of
humanity: one was the invention of the alphabet – writing
down *sounds* instead of words and thus making it possible
to write down any word in any language with about two
dozen signs – and the invention of the wheel. For an
advanced, industrial civilisation, like the Japanese, to do
without the alphabet is almost as anomalous as it would be
to do without the wheel.

The precise number of the ideographs taken over cannot be stated but it must be around five thousand. Some of them consist of one stroke; the most complicated of twenty-three strokes. If you put one stroke wrong, the meaning is lost or changed. It may take a child weeks to learn a single one of the complicated characters; or – put it in another way – most of them will go through life without even coming across them.

For a few centuries after the eighth, the two languages, Chinese and Japanese, were identical in writing. The two people could read one another's books and letters but neither could understand one single word of the other's spoken language. (The relationship between Urdu and Hindi was exactly the opposite. In their case the spoken language was identical and they could converse without the slightest difficulty; but they could not read one single word from the other's books or letters because Urdu used the Arabic, Hindi the Sanskrit script.)

The original Chinese ideographs are the *kanji*. Japanese, however, went on developing in its own way and, before long, differences between the two tongues revealed inadequacies in *kanji* when used for Japanese. New words came into use; new ideas and new notions had to be written down and there were no *kanji* to denote them. There were also the difficulties with foreign names. Obviously there was no *kanji* for *Shakespeare, Praxiteles* or *Hindenburg*. So what to do? The Japanese helped themselves by inventing two *syllabaries*. The Japanese language is quite melodious, it does not tolerate accumulation of consonants. Every syllable consists either of a single vowel or a combination of a vowel and a consonant. No word (or name) can end on a consonant, with the exception of *n* (remember *san*, for instance). As a result of this the language has about four dozen syllables. Scholars invented the *kana: katakana* and *hiragana*, signs denoting all the syllables of the language. *Katakana* is used to write down foreign words and names, and to italicise words, while *hiragana* is used for those Japanese words and such Japanese names which cannot be written down in *kanji*. Both syllabaries are very old: *katakana* was invented in the eighth, *hiragana* in the ninth century. There is an interesting story attached to *hiragana*. It was originated by a Buddhist saint, called Kobo Daishi. He wrote a charming little poem, using all *hiragana* syllables once – but never repeating any one of them. The translation of this *hiragana* poem is this: 'All is transitory in this fleeting world. Let me escape from its illusions and vanities.'*

In the olden days any amount of *kanji* ideographs could be used and high-brow writers, to show off their immense knowledge, always used as many complicated ideographs as they could dig up. Reading became more and more difficult, endless suffering in fact, but that was the reader's funeral. The main thing seemed to be not that he should understand but that he should be impressed by the author's erudition. Nevertheless, second thoughts eventually prevailed and writers started to put next to the more complicated *kanji* an explanation of its meaning, in tiny print and in a *fourth* system, called *funigara*. A Japanese scholar of an earlier generation remarked ruefully: 'A system of writing which is a combination of three systems and yet needs a fourth to explain itself, is easily the most inferior in the world.'

Four systems seem to be quite a handful; but that is not all. There are ancient, obsolete ideographs understood only by specialists. While walking in the garden of a Kyoto temple with an extremely intelligent pupil of Kyoto University I asked him what an inscription meant. He glanced at

* *Instant Japanese*, by Masahiro Watanabe and Kei Nagashima, Yohan Publications.

it and said: 'No idea. Old-fashioned writing.' The truth is that Egyptian hieroglyphics are a simple way of writing down one's thoughts compared with Japanese, which has four alphabets in theory and none in practice.

The Japanese did not remain unaware of these disadvantages and in 1948 they instituted reforms to simplify their writing. They chose two simplified sets of ideographs: eight hundred and eighty-one was chosen for a not too well educated but large layer of the population who stopped going to school at sixteen. Simple books, tales, romances, women's magazines etc. – i.e. a vast literature is printed in these selected *kanji* plus *kana*.

This, however, was not enough for a proper vocabulary so a second compromise was reached. Another set of 1,850 ideographs (including the eight hundred and eighty-one) was chosen for ordinary newspapers, books and general literature, and now these 1,850 are almost universally used. There was a great linguistic controversy: some people said essential ideographs were discarded while silly, useless ones were retained. But it is like an anthology: one man's selection is nobody else's, and one could argue till doomsday why one poem was included while another was left out. Whatever the merits of the selection, only these 1,850 *kanji* are used in modern publications. This, with *kana*, means many more than 1,850 words. Because – to complicate their system a little further – the Japanese have combinations of two or three ideographs. One *kanji* may mean one thing, another a second thing, but the two together means a third thing. For example: one sign means *road;* another *railway line*; the two together means *strategy*.

The horrible drawbacks of this system are obvious.

(1) It takes a Japanese child about eleven years to learn to read and write properly, a terrible waste of energy and

ability which, in a sharply competitive world where brains are becoming the greatest treasure, Japan will not be able to afford indefinitely.

(2) No one, literally no one, knows all the ideographs. Scholars may come near enough to perfection but they will never reach it. At the other end of the scale there are millions who keep mixing up the ideographs – even the eight hundred and eighty-one – making the wrong strokes, writing one thing when they mean another. It's a question of strokes, not tones, but the same kind of mistake can be made: you may want to write 'Morning dew' and produce some unutterable vulgarity instead by putting a few strokes wrong. There are millions of people who cannot consult the telephone book properly. All Japanese telegrams are written out in *katakana* – a reasonable but unusual way – and there are countless people who receive urgent telegrams but cannot read them.

I must make it clear that learning the eight hundred and eighty-one or the 1,850 ideographs does not mean learning so many complicated, unconnected and illogical signs. There is a clever, logical system (mostly based on *radicals* – the same basic signs appearing in many words which are vague synonyms or belong to the same group) and thus the situation is that the more ideographs one knows the more one can learn with increasing ease. Radicals help one; but – as always in Japanese writing – they may also confuse one and make life a little more difficult. But even if the system is built on logic, it remains unwieldy and almost insuperable. Literacy in Japan is high, indeed, the highest in the world. There are no people who are completely illiterate; but there are no people who are fully literate either. Even great scholars, as I have said, are beaten by the odd *kanji*; or in other words, even the most learned come across words in their own language which they cannot read. A situation unimaginable in the case of a Swedish or Spanish child of average intelligence, above the age of seven.

(3) Because of these difficulties only very few foreigners learn Japanese and an already isolated language is condemned, by its script, to eternal isolation. Japanese writers can scarcely communicate with the rest of the world. Few Japanese know English or French well enough to translate *into* these languages; and if I put the number of first-class translators (Japanese and foreign-born) at a dozen, I am exaggerating vastly. Lucky or exceptional Japanese writers ↖ – a handful – may speak to the world; the rest are condemned to silence outside their own country.

The question arises: why don't they scrap the system and introduce something else? It is the Latin alphabet Westerners think of first. Of course, it goes against the grain to throw out a considerable part of your national heritage and see it go down the drain. No nation, however, is more accustomed to wiping its slate clean and starting anew than the Japanese. Besides, it is not the introduction of the Latin alphabet that is advocated, but the use of *kana*. *Kana* is eminently suited to their language, is actually in use and – unlike *kanji* – is their own invention, *the* truly Japanese script.

There is no great fight on; no movement presses hard for an immediate change. But the issue lurks in the background and is bound to be raised effectively sooner or later. Opponents of any change have mustered many arguments – the main being a sentimental attachment to the past and a natural objection to such thoroughgoing, unsettling reform.

(1) They say that if they used only *kana* no one would learn *kanji*, and the entire pre-reform literature of Japan would remain unread and would consequently die. It would have to be reset in *kana* for the sake of new generations.

The truth, however, is that the 1948 reforms condemned the old literature to partial death in any case. Few people know enough *kanji* to read the classics; the 1,850 signs are not enough to read an author who used 4,000. The only way to bring the classics to life in any case would be to reset them, either using the 1,850 signs or using *kana*. (A similar situation arose in Greece, years ago. The Greeks went on pretending for a long time that modern Greek was really ancient Greek with slight variations, so Sophocles, Euripides, Aristophanes, Plato etc, were never translated into modern Greek. The result of this pretence was that the Greek classics were read less in Greece than anywhere else. As soon as the reformists got their way and it was recognised that for a modern Greek to learn classical Greek was to learn a new language, and as soon as the classics *were* translated into modern Greek – set up in *kana*, so to say – they came to life again.)

In Japan the old classics are not reset in any way and remain unread except by a devoted and dedicated minority.

(2) It is also said that the advantages to be gained would be small. I can only mention one or two facts pointing to the contrary. Hardly anyone uses a typewriter in Japan. A Japanese typewriter is only slightly smaller than the Jodrell Bank radio-telescope, looks like a mixture of a computer and a self-propelled gun, but is a little more complex than either. The typewriter is so unpopular and unpractical that in most offices letters and documents are still scribbled out in long-hand and then xeroxed: this, in the second half of the twentieth century, in one of the most industrially advanced countries of the world.

Lynotype-machines, on the other hand, are surprisingly small, but they need a near-genius to operate them. He uses both hands and operates three or four pedals with his feet, and he can actually *make up* the 1,850 *kanji* he needs (and he also has *kana*). Proofs, however, have to be read four or five times.

(3) Conservatives say that *kana* would impoverish the language. In fact, it would enrich it. It is the use of 1,850 *kanji* which impoverishes Japanese – a very rich and expressive tongue. Where there are ten synonyms, only two may be used; rarer words have to be abandoned and they drop out of everyday use. *Kana* would stop the rot: everything can be written out in *kana* (as in telegrams everything *is* written out in *kana*) and everyone could use any word he pleased.

(4) The final argument is that Japanese has many homophones. Take the sentence: *hashi de tabemasu. Hashi* means 'I eat' and the whole sentence means 'I eat with chopsticks'. But it may also mean 'I eat on the bridge', and also 'I eat on the edge' (of something). When the sentence is written down all doubts disappear: the proper *kanji* makes the meaning clear.

I admit that certain Japanese scholars have a definite advantage over me: they know Japanese. Homophones, they told me, are much more frequent than in English and although few of these Japanese scholars knew English, I bow to that. Nevertheless homophones exist in English, too, so we are not unfamiliar with the problem. In any case, when a Japanese *speaks* no one knows which *kanji* he would use if he wrote his words down. His meaning must be made clear by the context. Take an English parallel. Imagine that Lord So-and-so who owns a stately home near Southend invited some people to stay with him and his guests brought their children with them. One of the children says: 'This morning we played hop-scotch on the pier.' This will be clear enough: they played hop-scotch on Southend pier. But suppose that the noble lord suddenly died that morning and the naughty children marked up his corpse and played hop-scotch on *it*. One of them could then say:

'This morning we played hop-scotch on the peer.' Only our own *kanjis* – writing either *pier* or *peer* – could make the speaker's meaning crystal clear. Yet it is no more common for real misunderstandings about homophones to arise in English speech than it is for naughty children to play hop-scotch on dead peers.

Kana is a good syllabary; it is purely Japanese (while *kanji* is not); it is more than a thousand years old. The Koreans are dropping *kanji* soon and will use *kana* only (their own version of *kana*) very soon and the Japanese too will have to take the plunge. No nation – certainly no leading industrial nation – can squander eleven years of its children's lives just learning the two r's. No modern nation can afford to risk that after those eleven years most of the children – except the most brilliant ones – should be able to say: 'I have spent eleven years learning the ideographs but I can proudly claim that after all this time I can neither read nor write properly.'

Nonsensu

You listen to Japanese and do not understand one single word of it. You may not know Finnish nor Arabic either, but listening to these two languages you will pick up an occasional word here and there, words like *democracy*, or *football* or *terrorist*, and you may jump to the conclusion that they are, or might be, discussing democracy, football or terrorists. Nothing like this will happen while listening to Japanese: you will not get one single word of it. Yet you know that Japanese is as predatory a language as English: it snatches words where it can. Indeed, Japanese purists are up in arms against the invasion of foreign words. But where are the invaders?

The answer is that the Japanese take the words and then twist them, adapt them, beyond recognition.

As no Japanese word can end on a consonant – they just cannot pronounce it that way – they add a vowel to the end of every borrowed word. Cheese, as I have mentioned, becomes *cheesu*; my name, in no time, became *Mikeshu;* and nonsense – a fully naturalized word in Japanese – becomes *nonsensu.*

In *nonsensu* the first two syllables end on *n*, so they are pronounceable. When one syllable of a foreign word ends on a consonant, a vowel is inserted: desk becomes *desuku*. They cannot pronounce *l*'s (they say *r*'s instead). London in Japanese becomes *Rondon*. (The Chinese do exactly the opposite. When a Chinese speaks English he will say *lice* meaning rice; a Japanese will speak of *fright* meaning flight.) Hotel in Japanese becomes *hoteru*. They have no *f* sound before an *e*, so coffee becomes *kohi*. Little wonder you cannot pick up the English words in Japanese when restaurant becomes *resutoran*, high-class (an accepted and much-used term) becomes *hai kurasu* and sandwich *sando* (an abbreviation, on top of it all): strike is *sutodaiko* (*suto* for short) and an engine-stop (a stall) an *ensto*. All these are *English* words.

In Japan people keep giving you their cards when you first meet them and I collected about three dozen cards every day. As it would have been most discourteous to throw them away, I have bought a special air-travel bag for cards and I shall keep my vast collection – even if I don't look at it ever again – till the end of my days. But perhaps I shall look at them, because it is always amusing to study them: one side is in English (name, occupation, address), the other in Japanese. It is, of course, the Japanese side which repays study. You point at a name and ask a Japanese friend what it is. He will say: Mountain Rice Paddy.

'Mountain rice paddy?' you ask slightly surprised. 'But it is Mr Yamada's card.'

'Quite. But Yamada means Mountain Rice Paddy.'

Many of the popular Japanese names mean something: *Ishibashi* means 'stone-bridge', *Nakamura* means 'inside the village' and *Mitsui* means 'three wells'. This is the same as in English. Some names (Young, Barber, Winterbottom) mean something, others (Bing, Shackleton, Cholmondeley) mean nothing. Both English and Japanese names may have their complications, but they are of a different kind. In English you have the name Cholmondeley or Maugham and you tell people that you pronounce it Chumley and

Maum and they will either remember it or not. In Japanese, however, you may write the names which have a meaning either in *kana* or in *kanji*. (Here I may remark that the Japanese post-war simplification of writing began with the sacred vow: no more new *kanji*. This was put into practice by introducing fifty new *kanji* only for names.)

The same ideograph, in many cases, may be read in the Japanese or in the Chinese way. It is – needless to say – more U to read it in the Chinese way. Ordinary people read their names in the Japanese way because to read them in the Chinese way would be pretentious and 'above their station', but when a man becomes truly eminent, they suddenly start to read his name in the Chinese way. The writing remains the same but the pronunciation changes. Hirobumi Ito was Hirobumi for most of his life; when he became Prime Minister in 1885 he suddenly became Hakubun.

That a man should change his name on becoming Prime Minister sounds hilarious to us. As soon as I get back to London, I'll tell this story to Lord Home – sorry, he became Sir Alec Douglas-Home on becoming Prime Minister – and we shall have a jolly good laugh together at those quaint Japanese.

Japanese is an extremely difficult language. There are a hundred ways of saying 'I'. 'There are different "I's" for men and women, young and old, city folk and country folk, members of good families and those of lowly families; different "I's" used according to situations (such as among friends, addressing subordinates or superiors); special "I's" that one uses in correspondence; and "I's" used in different ages of the past.'* *Rice* means rice on a plate, served in the Western way; *gohan* is Japanese rice, always served in

---

* Watanabe and Nagashima, *op. cit.*

E   129

a bowl. Iron is *kane* but real ladies must never say *kane*
(I never heard that *kane* was a dirty word in any other
language; but it is undeniably a four-letter word in
Japanese) – real ladies must call it *okane*. And so forth. I
could go on for hours. What can a foreigner do?

He can choose between two possibilities. He can take the
risk of saying *garasu* (pane-glass) when he really means
gurasu (drinking glass) – both words coming from *glass*; he
can refer to himself with an 'I' denoting a man of good
family although he, as a *gaijin*, is a man of lowly origin;
he can make a variety of other equally absurd mistakes, and
hope to be understood and forgiven. Or again he can
surmount these difficulties and learn Japanese perfectly.
Perfectly is perhaps too high a claim. Many Japanese and
Japanese-speaking foreigners told me that a ninety per cent
knowledge is the maximum attainable to a *gaijin*. (Most
Japanese will know less of their own language, but their
mistakes will be of a different kind.)

It is when the rare foreigner has achieved this ninety
per cent (or even a slightly lower) status that his real
troubles begin. An American friend, a brilliant Japanese
scholar, told me: 'They are absolutely convinced that no
foreigner can speak proper Japanese. Pidgin-Japanese, with
a few odd words, well that's quite touching and polite; but
the legend is that no foreigner can progress beyond that.
So when I speak to them in perfect Japanese they are
foxed. They look at me in bewilderment and think that *I
have spoken English*. As they know that they cannot speak
English they are sure they have failed to understand me.
If they do speak English they understand me but think I
have spoken English to them and they reply in English. I
go to the station every day and ask for my ticket in Japanese.
The clerk – and a different clerk on each occasion – may not
look up at me at all. If he doesn't there is no trouble. I
ask for my ticket in Japanese, he gives it to me as he does

to all other passengers and on I go. But if he looks up, he either answers me in English – believing that that was the language I addressed him in – or he is simply unable to understand what I want until I repeat my request in English. On the telephone I have no difficulty whatever. But in the streets, in shops, in offices I may go up to a person, address him in perfect Japanese and get the courteous reply: "Sorry, I don't speak English." In restaurants I order something in Japanese and the flabbergasted waiter turns to my Japanese wife: if she nods, endorsing my order, it is accepted. Once in Hokkaido I had a different reaction. I went to a place where perhaps they had never seen a *gaijin* before. I spoke to a man in Japanese and, surprisingly, he understood every word I said. He took me for a Japanese. When I finished, instead of answering my question, he asked me in bewilderment: "But why did you dye your hair blond?" '

More educated people, of course, realise the dreadful fact: some *gaijin* can speak good Japanese. And they do not like it. The *gaijin* should speak English. To speak any other language is wrong. Japanese should speak Japanese; foreigners should speak English. For a foreigner to speak Japanese is intrusion on their privacy; it is eavesdropping. It's Commodore Perry's steamships on the spiritual horizon once again.

On the other hand, millions of Japanese learn English with dedication and diligence. I met quite a few people who get up at five o'clock every morning to listen to the English lesson on the radio. The demand for English teachers is so high that people who spent two days in London or New York and have less than a smattering of English can get jobs as teachers. I met English teachers whom I would reject even as pupils – they were hopeless cases. No English-speaking person can fail to get a reasonably good job in Japan today as a teacher, interpreter or translator.

Many signs and notices are put up in English, and teachers who really know English are employed to word them. Over an elegant shop I saw the neon-sign:

LADIES OUTFATTERS

'It's not fair to laugh,' I rebuked myself. 'A mistake of the sign-maker. The person who worded it most certainly knew how to spell the word.'

He most certainly did. As I got nearer, I saw another, smaller sign with an arrow:

LADIES CAN HAVE FITS UPSTAIRS

The Fragile Giant

Ask a Japanese any question and G.N.P. – Gross National Product – will somehow creep into the answer. Be the question about golf, or the weather or the railway time-table between Nagoya and Osaka, the reply will somehow be connected with G.N.P. What *bushido* and the national flag used to be in former times, G.N.P. is today. Before going to Japan I did not even know that there was such a thing as G.N.P.; by the time I left, I had come to believe that there was nothing else.

It is trying, even exasperating, for the poor Briton to read day by day on the front page of Japanese newspapers that exports have reached new heights, that the balance of payment has further improved, that new orders from abroad are pouring in, that the Tokyo stock-exchange (having been in the doldrums for eight years) is reaching new, undreamt-of peaks – and then to see, on an inside page, that Upper Clyde shipbuilders report a loss of £10.3m; that new, catastrophic trade-figures have been published in Britain but the Government has explained that these figures do not mean that the economy is not buoyant: the bad figures are simply due to (1) increased imports, (2) the New York dock strike and (3) the devaluation of the Argentine peso.

I was foolish enough to ask for economic pamphlets, book-lets, statistics and surveys from various Tokyo ministries, universities and economic institutions. The result was a flood of excellent documents, several tons of them, trumpet-ing abroad the Great Achievement and lauding the glorious G.N.P. Here is the briefest summary of this breath-taking success story: G.N.P. (no, you cannot get away from it) was £7,000 million in 1952, when occupation ended, and is £48,000 million today – an increase of nearly seven hundred per cent. Japan's steel production is third after the United States and the Soviet Union; Japan is the leading ship-building nation of the world and the second largest automobile producer. More and more people are better off every year; holiday resorts are crowded; rooms in Western-style hotels as well as in *ryokans*, Japanese inns, are more and more difficult to book; and the department stores are doing a roaring trade. One Sunday before Christmas 1967, Mitsukoshi, one of the largest popular stores, took £820,000, nearly two million dollars. Almost every family has a tele-vision set and colour sets are gaining popularity at tremend-ous speed. Proportionately more families have refrigerators and washing machines than in Britain.

How has the Japanese Miracle been achieved? There were three main factors: (1) hard work and ingenuity; (2) good luck, and (3) a trait which could be politely described as enlightened self-interest, mystically as *sacro egoismo* and more outspokenly as ruthless selfishness.

(1) There is no doubt that the Japanese have worked very hard indeed; their success was mostly – although not en-tirely – in return for their sweat, blood and labour. Their labour-force is educated and literate and second to none in intelligence. Economy is the new patriotism of the Japanese and they are very patriotic people. Long Live G.N.P. The workers are as proud of it as the capitalists

are. The labour force is loyal to its firms, and labour relations are good. There is a real team-spirit, the workers *belong;* occasionally, when one hears that even their marriages are arranged by the firms, one has the vague feeling that they not only *belong* but simply *belong to* the firms.

This does not mean that Trade Unions are not powerful. There are great wage-battles every spring, led by the two politically organised groups: *Sohyo,* of the left, and *Domei,* a middle-of-the-road organisation. Lightning strikes (lasting as a rule for five or six hours) are ordered, but mainly as bargaining tactics, just to bare the Unions' teeth. Occasionally bitter and extremely unpleasant disputes with strong political undertones flare up.

All this, however, is on the national level. Life within the individual firms is happier, sometimes idyllic. Trade Unions are organised within every firm: all workers and clerical staff, including directors, belong to one Union. Individual strikes against one single employer are rare. There are no demarcation disputes: as only one union exists per firm, there can be no dispute with another union. As all people are members of the same organisation, from the office boy up to the managing director, there is no 'bloody manager', no 'we' and 'they'. They all work for the company, for the same aim. As this aim is to raise production and not to raise profits, the workers' enthusiasm can be more easily kindled. Profit is a dirty word while 'production' is semi-sacred, second only to G.N.P. The workers can share in the glory of production; they do not share – not directly, anyway – in the profits.

Prices do rise but wages rise more quickly. This, of course, should keep everybody happy; but it does not – for reasons to be explained presently.

(2) Japan has had good luck. First, she lost the war and before losing it her industry was, fortunately, destroyed. This is no facetious remark or frivolous joke, but a sober

assessment, shared by most Japanese economists. Of course the loss of the war meant a great deal of suffering, humiliation and tragedy; but it also made efficient rebuilding much easier. Japan had to start from scratch and received all the help she needed. Without the war and the destruction which followed in its wake, Japanese industry could not possibly be half as up-to-date as it is.

That was World War Two. Further wars meant further strokes of luck. The Korean War was a godsend, coming just at the right moment. It was fought on Japan's doorstep and money galore poured in. The blessings of the Korean War had not even been fully counted when the Americans – Japan's best friends – obliged with the Vietnam War, another huge source of income.

(3) The third factor is Japan's selfishness. After World War Two Japan paid voluntarily – bilaterally negotiated – reparation to her former enemies, the Philippines, Indonesia, Burma, etc. This was decency rather than selfishness, one may object. That's true; but there was a great deal of foresight and clever calculation involved. These reparations were paid in goods. Afterwards Japan helped the underdeveloped Asian countries, also by sending them goods. At first, the Japanese were hated and resented, but people got used to them; permanent contact on a man-to-man basis convinced these former enemies that the Japanese were honest, likeable people. The Australians used to loathe them; they are fully accepted in Australia today. Before they knew where they were, they got used to Japanese goods; Japanese firms were solidly entrenched on their soil; Japan did a roaring trade with them. Another economic blessing of the lost war. Trade, in this case, did not follow the pious missionary; it followed the penitent pacifist.

Japanese goods are competitive today because the workers are still paid low wages. Wages have undoubtedly risen but they started from rock bottom. Japanese wages today are half of European wages and one third of United States wages. Prices are twenty per cent cheaper than in Europe and thirty-five per cent cheaper than in the United States, so the Japanese worker is worse off than either his European or American counterparts. It is largely these low wages which help Japanese goods to be internationally competitive. (Social insurance has also improved lately but the whole system is far inferior to the British National Health Service and Japanese workers are much worse off in this respect too.)

Japan is also one of the most protectionist countries in the world. Japanese industry still plays the part of the little boy who has recently started from scratch and needs very gentle treatment. They cannot let foreign competitors in because their industry is too fragile. If it is, it is a fragile giant; a gentle bulldozer; a feeble bull in the china-shop. The motor-car industry is the worst of the lot; but in every field the Japanese make concessions to foreign competitors only when their own export is threatened – and even then always the minimum concessions. Every advantage which they are never slow to claim for themselves – such as, say, landing rights of foreign aircraft – has to be fought for tooth and nail and is resisted to the last ditch. Japan claims all rights and facilities for her own exports but she has discovered that it is better to sell than buy; better to export than to import; better to make money than to spend it. Perhaps the same thoughts have – at least *en passant* – occurred to other nations too, but they know better by now. This is Japan's first taste of true prosperity: she was used to being a poor country all her life. Japan can still get away with her pose of weakness, particularly in America where the guilt of the atom-bomb still lingers on. So poor little Japan – the third largest industrial power in the world – has to be helped and nursed by economic giants like Britain and France.

Does all that mean that Japan is a happy, carefree country? I am afraid it does not. Wages have risen but the wages structure is still not much higher than in Venezuela. The standard of living – notwithstanding the number of washing machines – is still much below that of Britain. Tokyo is growing into an uncontrollable mess and traffic – on road and rail – is becoming impossible. The life of commuters (and there are millions of them) is hell. (The railways employ professional *pushers*. These men stand on the platforms, charge the mass of humanity and by sheer force of kinetic energy squeeze a dozen or two extra sardines into the railway carriage. Perhaps a few dozen are squeezed out on the other side but no one would miss them.) Roads, as soon as you get off the superhighways with their impressive and spectacular intersections are pretty awful. The housing shortage is frightening and as more agricultural labourers flood into the cities it is getting worse : there is no privacy, overcrowding is dreadful. Only about twenty per cent of Japanese houses have proper drainage, the honey-cart still trots along the streets even of Tokyo at night. Noise is constant and deafening. Air pollution is poisonous.

The Economic Planning Agency on Japanese Living Standards prepared a White Paper for the government and, among other things, reported (according to *The Times,* July 7, 1969) that to judge by the number of parks in Japanese cities and the availability of public libraries, Japan rates far behind the advanced countries of the West. The United States is fifteen times better off in this respect.

There is a great deal of dissatisfaction about these problems. The Agency implied that the government ought to pay more attention to the lot of the common man and less to the economic glory of Japan as reflected in – guess what – G.N.P.

Over one third of the working people complained that their budgets were severely strained. Even though incomes

were increasing every year, people did not feel much better off. The rich also complain about the unbearable traffic conditions: that they cannot drive 'their new Toyotas and Nissans through the heavy traffic in cities'.

The Prime Minister's Office had previously published evidence that 'frustration indices' existed on an unprecedented level. 'Frustration index' is just American semi-scientific jargon meaning that a sense of frustration is spreading among the Japanese. This does not prove, of course, that the Economic Miracle is non-existent or is not a real miracle. But the more a Japanese hears about it, the more he expects for himself. Propaganda is counter-productive: the greater the glory of Japan, the higher individual expectations become and the worse the frustration. All this should not cause ironic smiles at the expense of the Japanese, we should feel no *schadenfreude*. Their achievement is great and awe-inspiring. Frustration only means that however much has been achieved a great deal still has to be done. It also brings home the lesson that man does not live by Economic Miracle alone.

It is not only the West which watches Japan, but also the new African nations. A member of the Japanese Government told me:

'They are in two minds. They feel contempt for us and say that after one single defeat we surrendered completely to the West. That we gave up all our aims and aspirations to pursue material welfare only – selfishly, egotistically and thinking of ourselves alone. But other, knowledgeable Africans wink. They imply: just wait. As soon as Japan is really strong enough, she will discard her veil and will reveal herself as a powerful ally and champion of the non-Western nations.'

My informant failed to add his own comment on the knowledgeable African wink. But Japan, of course, will not discard her veil; she *has* no veil. Japan is not the champion of the East; nor of the West; of the non-aligned; nor of the aligned. She is the champion of herself. And this, perhaps, is the strongest and most powerful basic reason for the frustration: the Japanese – workers, capitalists and particularly students – feel that the rich have only one great, noble and sacred aim: to become even richer.

And they ask (in Japanese this is a more elegant phrase, with a distinct archaic flavour); *so what?*

Paradise

Japan is the world's greatest expense account Paradise. Salaries, like wages, are still comparatively low; salaries, in fact, have risen less sharply than wages. The average salary of a clerk is Y 40,000 a month which comes to £560 or $1,350 *per annum*. But a lot of perks, fringe benefits, change the picture. Large bonuses are paid twice a year, raising the man's money income considerably; travel to and from work is usually paid for; people get free or subsidised lunches; unmarried employees often get free housing; married and unmarried get free holidays with all expenses paid; and there are, usually, excellent sporting and other leisure facilities. And ultimately, when the man reaches the stratospheric heights of the expense account world, he reaches heaven. His life is changed. He can take clients, visitors, inquirers out for lunch or dinner, sign the bill and forget about it.

This 'go and enjoy yourself' is a traditional attitude of Japanese employers: it is paternalistic like almost everything in Japan. The gay and dazzling entertainment world of the Ginza and other places is a wonderful escape after hard work but even this escape is arranged for you by the company. And even during your escape you continue working for the company. Elegant and fashionable places are ruinously expensive. On their salary alone none of them could get near them; as it is, they live in them. The places are full and not one single bill is paid from an individual's pocket – unless a stray American vice-president happens to walk in, but his bill, in turn, will probably be presented to *his* company.

If you are taken out by your Japanese host in the evening you will be taken to several places. After a sumptuous dinner he will take you to a fabulous – although probably a shade too noisy – night-club where hostesses will be invited to the table. These ladies drink a lot (often yellow-tinted water which will pass – as far as the bill is concerned – for whisky) and they also get high table-money. Your host will often invite *two* hostesses for each male guest. Japanese hospitality is fabulous; but the idea never far from their minds is that the other chap has to be impressed: 'We can afford it'.

All this is entirely at the tax-payers' expense. Every penny – as long as you have the bill – is deductible. Japan's entertainment bill is larger than many an Asian country's total budget; and it is frequently pointed out by rueful Americans, who are responsible for Japan's defence, that the Japanese treasury spends more on dinners, night-clubs and geisha-girls than on defence.

There is a festival in June when fireflies, or fire-bugs, are said to bring luck. But Tokyo has no fireflies so plane-loads of 'luck' have to be imported from Hokkaido. A country where bugs travel by aeroplane must be prosperous indeed; and one where they travel at the tax-payers' expense, many would say, must be Paradise itself.

Westerners often suggest that there is a great deal of corruption in Japanese entertainment. Perhaps it is only a different interpretation of the idea of corruption, but certain practices certainly do seem unusual to us; although – this must be emphasised – all is done openly and above board. A man may be employed, in an executive capacity and with a high salary, by one of the large companies and his only duty will be to cultivate and entertain the firm's banker on whom even more depends in Japan than in Britain or the United States. This official will have to play golf with the banker, and take him out to restaurants, night-clubs, geisha-houses, and for week-ends. This is not regarded as bribery either by the firm or by the bank: the two are supposed to discuss business, and no doubt business must be one of many subjects that crop up.

It is quite customary for the head of a government department to entertain the head of another government department to a slap-up meal, in order to discuss government business. A few advisers are usually included on both sides. And the invitation is always promptly and generously reciprocated.

Women are nearly always excluded from all this – even on occasions when a foreign visitor brings his wife. Japanese women do not seem to mind very much, although one can hear more rebellious murmuring today than a few years ago. But on the whole Japanese women *expect* their husbands to stay out late, to take people out, to go to geisha-houses (and behave virtuously while there although few questions are asked). Busy evenings mean that the husband is successful and is getting ahead; if he can spend too many evenings in his happy family circle he has surely failed in his job.

Like everything else in Japan, entertainment is strictly hierarchical. Who entertains whom, where, and how much he is allowed to spend is carefully weighed. At first I was a little embarrassed by the hospitality lavished upon me, until I understood that I was just as much a gift of God to them as they were a gift of God to me: I was raw material, an excuse for them to go out. Entertainable guests who look reasonably acceptable on the expense accounts are few and far between; when they turn up there is keen competition for them.

I learnt, too, that I – like everyone else – had been graded and assessed in advance and from that moment I jealously watched the places we went to and – whenever I could do so without disgrace – threw a discreet glance at the bill when it was being signed. I was greatly flattered one evening when, taken out by a company vice-president, I saw that the bill for the two of us ran to Y 50,000 (nearly £60 or $140), which was about my host's monthly salary. But I was duly put in my place next day when I heard that on the same night the President himself entertained a Dutch tycoon – a businessman who really mattered, and not a mere writer – and *their* bill, including a geisha-house to which I was not taken, came to Y 150,000 (£180 or $425). There was nothing extraordinary in this. It was just an ordinary evening out for the President. Nothing is really too much for the Japanese tax-payer.

Big firms also give lavish parties, sometimes to several thousand guests. All of them receive a gift at the end. I saw only two of these gifts. One was a set of encyclopaedias – about twenty-four volumes for each guest; the other was a tape-recorder.

A big Japanese firm does not think twice before inviting you over to Japan for a discussion, or to give a lecture or just to look around. First class air-ticket, a suite in a luxury hotel and all your expenses paid.

A witty and cosmopolitan businessman-friend, who was also frank, told me once that he was due to go soon on an exciting journey to South East Asia with a fat travel allowance. He looked forward to the journey, especially to Hong Kong and Thailand, because he was mad about Chinese and Thai women. But he was also worried. He had crossed his company's President and feared his revenge. It was a very Japanese affair, no argument, no unpleasantness, no open disagreement. All that happened was that the President suggested something at a meeting and my friend asked him, most courteously, if another way of doing it had also been considered. This was nearly open rebellion and he was worried lest his trip be cancelled on some feeble excuse to teach him a lesson for the future.

One evening he came to meet me, half amused, half furious.

'The bastard . . .' he fumed.

'What is it?' I asked.

'My trip, of course.'

'He cancelled it?'

'Oh no. I'm going all right.'

'He cut your allowance?'

'No. That's the whole point. The cunning old bastard. He doubled it.'

'???'

'So that I should be able to take my wife.'

Politics

Japan runs true to form. Even in the old days she was accustomed to political chaos coupled with economic prosperity. Today she is more prosperous than ever before; and instead of chaos she is plagued with or enjoys – political oblivion. As a military power Japan is non-existent: she renounced war; as an international political factor she does not count. If Mao growls or the Indian Prime Minister dismisses one of her ministers, it is front page news the world over: if there are fights and fisticuffs in Japan's parliament people read a brief paragraph about it, yawn and turn the page. Mao Tse Tung and Mrs Gandhi are household names; but how many people know the name of Japan's Premier?

Japan's nationalism is economic nationalism and there is nothing new about this, except that it is militarily non-aggressive. Yet we resent this slightly, as if Japan had less right to trade and succeed than we do (except, of course, that we don't). Japan, in turn, indignantly resents the suggestion that this economic nationalism exists, as if it were a grave accusation and not the only possible – and most innocent – outlet for a great and proud nation.

Japan is a democracy established on an Anglo-American pattern by a new Constitution promulgated in 1947. The Diet consists of two Houses: the House of Representatives (the Lower House with four hundred and eighty-six seats) and the House of Councillors (the Upper House, with two-hundred and fifty seats). Members of both Houses are elected, on different suffrage. Members of the House of Representatives are elected for four years, of the House of Councillors for six (with one half of them elected every three years). Voting age begins at twenty and women – contrary to all expectations – have the vote. Indeed, they make good use even of their passive votes: there are seven women in the House of Representatives and sixteen in the 'other place'. Since the end of the war there have been no attempts to establish a personal or group dictatorship. Without any such attempt, however, it is the *zaibatsu* – the business interests – who gently advise and guide the government. In a country where economics are the only vital interest many people regard this as fair and sensible. Others allege that the *zaibatsu* is a nameless clique of back-room boys, responsible to no one and unknown to the public, so the arrangement is neither fair nor sensible. Whichever side is right, no unbiased observer can say that there is a businessmen's dictatorship in Japan and that string-pulling in the background is more rife than in any other democratic country one could name.

In 1885 Prince Hirobumi Ito formed Japan's first parliamentary government; Mr Eisaku Sato formed its sixty-second in parliamentary history and the seventeenth since the adoption of the New Constitution.

This New Constitution, in addition to establishing a proper, working democracy in Japan, contains two remarkable special articles.

One of them established a principle which is commonplace all over the world, and which therefore passed almost unnoticed; the other introduced a unique principle and has therefore attracted a great deal of attention.

According to the New Constitution the Prime Minister can dismiss all his ministers. What could be more natural than that? – readers may ask. What indeed? But in the twenties and thirties there was *one* minister the Premier could not dismiss: and this single undismissible member was the Minister of War. It was always the Army who 'gave' a Minister of War to the government. Had one been dismissed the Army would have refused to supply a new Minister of War, a grave constitutional crisis would have arisen and the formation of a government would have been impossible. It was this rule which assured the Army's domination over the government (a much more sinister domination than that of the *zaibatsu* today). But for the rule mentioned, the Manchurian incident and the Chinese adventure – always resisted and disapproved by the government, always planned and forced upon them by the Army, through the Minister of War – would have been impossible and Japan's modern history might have been very different. Her recent past would have been better; her present would be worse.

The other provision is widely known. Article 9 of the 1947 Constitution declares that 'the Japanese people forever renounce war as a sovereign right of the people' and land, sea and air forces are forbidden. The Americans rejoiced when this paragraph was accepted. It is said to be General MacArthur's own brainchild and one of his greatest personal triumphs. The United States undertook full responsibility for Japan's defence. Today the Americans would like to persuade Japan to rearm, at least to a small extent. Japan does only as much as suits her: she does have some land, sea and air forces. A Constitution can be interpreted in many ways. But these forces are tiny and could not protect Japan against any foe. The Americans think Japan ought to have greater forces. The Germans have kindly agreed to rearm, why not the Japanese? But Japan does not

149

oblige; she shakes her head and replies: '*Tu l'a voulu Georges Dandin,*' – it was your own idea, why complain because your heartfelt wishes have been fulfilled? To leave the defence of Japan to the United States is true to Japan's original, sacred promise; it is much more virtuous. And also much, much cheaper.

It is also much more sensible and logical. As long as we have two super-powers which keep the balance of terror – or call it the peace of the world – by the Second Striking Force, by the 'dead man's revenge' – in other words through the fear of one that the other can effectively retaliate even after a most devastating and successful attack – it is more realistic to rely on one of these super-powers than to speak of 'independent nuclear deterrents'. Not only more realistic but, I repeat, much, much cheaper. You cannot really compare the prices of the two.

The situation of Britain and Japan, so similar in many respects, seems to be the reverse in this one. But that's only how it appears at first glance. Japan is economically strong but politically insignificant; while Britain is economically weak but still has a great deal of political influence all over the world. This is true; but the point discussed is defence. Britain (said Mr Khrushchev) could be completely destroyed by three hydrogen bombs and France by four. Japan would probably need another four. Japan could not retaliate after an attack by hydrogen bombs but neither could Britain or France. It is not our Bomb that protects us but the knowledge that should we be attacked, the United States could and would retaliate – irrespective of whether she herself had been attacked too or not. In other words, Britain – whatever our illusions – is in exactly the same position as Japan: our defence *is* left to the United States. Japan grows rich but she has no effective deterrent; we grow poor, ruined by defence expenditure, and have no effective deterrent either. As Miss Sophie

Tucker, one of the brightest if not one of the most distinguished philosophers of these decades, has said: 'I've been
poor, I've been rich. Rich is better.'

A few words on Japan's political parties. The country is
ruled by the Liberal Democratic Party, founded in 1955
from a merger of various conservative groups. The ruling
party is conservative, a friend and ally of the Americans;
it is anti-Communist, and both supports and is supported by
big business. As the United States is Japan's good friend
and protector; as the country is doing well and the standard
of living is going up by leaps and bounds; and as the Communists across the water cannot be completely ignored,
most people are inclined to believe that Sato's policy –
although debatable on points of detail – is the only sensible
one. 'What's wrong with this government?' people ask. Perhaps the only trouble is that it's deadly dull. The Japanese
feel frustrated and long for political excitement. The United
States is an excellent target. You are always more irritated
by your true friends than by your enemies. And Okinawa,
as we have seen, is a remarkably good issue to become
excited over, from extreme left to extreme right.

President Nixon knows that too. He has said that in the
new Security Treaty he would be ready to undertake to
return Okinawa in 1972.

The Japanese Socialist Party was also founded in 1955,
under the Chairmanship of Mr Mosaburo Suzuki. Although
the Party was the reunification of left-wing and right-wing
Socialists who had been split for years, today it
follows a left-wing line. It is strongly anti-American and
keeps making attempts to take the wind out of the Communist sails. It tries to gain the support of young people
by protesting against the new Security Treaty, but loses

this support almost before gaining any because it condemns violence.

The Japanese Communist Party tried to maintain neutrality between the Soviet Union and China as long as possible. When this proved impossible, it split into pro-Chinese and pro-Soviet factions. Its skilful leaders have managed, in the end, to patch things up and establish some measure of independence. They do not identify themselves with either great Communist power but follow their own interests. This does not endear them to either: they were not represented at the Moscow summit. They are an important political force but numerically not a great party. They have about 300,000 members and five seats in the Diet. Seventy per cent of the Party's members are under forty. Marxism-Leninism, like all full and closely reasoned systems, has always had a magnetic attraction for many Japanese; on the other hand the brutal and treacherous occupation of Czechoslovakia was a bitter blow to the Party's popularity.

The most interesting Party on the scene is the Komeito. It is the political arm of the Soka Gakkai, a religious group of the Nicheren Sect of Buddhism. The Party advocates a welfare state, talks in vague but appealing terms about humanity and a human type of Socialism, about cleaning up political life, about making democracy really democratic and about other generalities. Its appeal is great; it is an unknown quantity and a much feared force. Ever since its foundation in 1964 it has set a target for itself before parliamentary and municipal elections and has always reached its target. In the last Diet it had twenty-five members, the Socialists had thirty-one. The most curious thing about Komeito is that its programme is so mystical, semi-religious and vague, that no one really knows whether it is a right-wing or a left-wing force. (Mr Sato ordered new elections in the last days of the 'sixties, and won an overwhelming victory. The Socialist Party went into eclipse, and the mysterious Komeito, with its lack of programme, doubled its size. So did the Communists. The moral: Japan seems to support the American alliance. But it should also be remembered that the elections were followed with apathy, and only about two-thirds of the electorate voted. Japan seems to be as bored with her politics as is the rest of the world.)

Japan's foreign policy is conspicuous by its non-existence. Japan always used to back up her foreign policy by force. Today she has no force; consequently she has no foreign policy. It all amounts to a neutrality which is, in fact, unilateral disarmament. Japan is content with this; she is quite ready to go on manufacturing motor-cars and transistor radios, building ships and office blocks and leaving political glory to Mao, Tito and Wilson.

It is often whispered in the visitor's ear that Japan is not a real democracy because its political life is corrupt.

This is a *non sequitur*.

The country *is* a real democracy. The democratic game is played honestly and strictly according to the rules. Elections decide which party is to govern. Everyone can say what he likes, the press is free, no one is persecuted for his opinions and the opposition may attack the government as wildly as it pleases.

But there are certain phenomena which strike the Western observer as curious. Voters are often paid. To their credit, this makes little difference. People accept the money and vote according to their conscience – another great advantage of the secret ballot. To be a politician is a fruitful career, indeed, good business. They are among the best paid politicians in the world; they can keep two secretaries at public expense; they are given luxurious houses – often with swimming pools – near the Diet; and they raise their

153

salaries with monotonous regularity. Business firms make large contributions not only to party funds but also to individuals and as these contributions are tax-free they do not have to be declared by the recipients. There are quite a few, exceedingly influential, pressure-groups. Another unusual feature of Japanese political life is that high-ranking civil servants often take up jobs on retirement with companies with whom they had official dealings in the past. A man may have been deciding for many years who gets building contracts and then become a director of one of those building firms who did not do too badly. Such arrangements need not *be* corrupt; but they certainly *look* corrupt. Nevertheless: they are made quite openly, and every appointment becomes public knowledge.

One day I had a dinner appointment with a high-ranking civil servant and I arrived a few minutes late. Apologising, I mentioned the name of the gentleman who had detained me. My host had never heard the name and asked me who he was.

'He used to be Ambassador to X and now is the vice-president of Y Oil Company.'

He thought this over seriously, perhaps with a view to his own future, then nodded earnestly: 'Not a bad promotion.'

Tolerance

Quite a few Japanese remarked to me with pride: 'We are completely free of racial prejudice.' This, more often than not, was after sessions in which they ran down their country and I defended it. They disapproved of almost everything around them, then concluded: 'But I must tell you one thing. There is absolutely no racial prejudice in Japan.'

To a great extent this is true. There is no anti-Armenian feeling because there are no Armenians. There is no anti-Semitism because there are no Japanese Jews. There are none of the anti-Greek sentiments you find in Istanbul and Alexandria, because there are no Greeks. There are no anti-Negro feelings because there are no Negroes. And there is not a trace of that anti-Bosnian prejudice which, I am told, was so regrettably prevalent in Herzegovina before 1908.

This is all to their credit. It is a fallacy to believe as I have just suggested – that you actually *need* minorities in order to be prejudiced against them, although, as is shown in Britain, it is of course *easier* to feel antagonistic to a minority if you have it. Britain used to be very proud of having no colour prejudice, and rather patronising vis-à-vis the United States because they didn't share this virtue. This was while Britain lacked coloured people, and today we hear little of this proud boast. On the other hand, Hitler

managed to work up a considerable number of his compatriots to a frenzy of homicidal fury against the Jews,
when the latter amounted to only one per cent of the
population, and the post-war Polish government did even
better: that frightened and bungling régime produced anti-
Semitism without any Jews at all. Nothing like this has
ever happened in Japan. All Bosnians are safe.

This 'complete lack of racial prejudice' rather worried
me. My main thesis had been that the Japanese are certainly not worse than we are; but not better either. They
are just human. And to be completely without racial
prejudice in this year of Our Lord is so virtuous as to be
inhuman. In the twenty-third century, perhaps; indeed,
most probably. But not today.

But I could relax. Racial prejudice is indeed not a national
problem – Japan is, after all, one of the racially most
homogeneous nations of the world – yet I am pleased to
report the following findings:

(1) I have already spoken about a slight anti-American
feeling which, however, is marginally different from the
anti-Americanism of, say, the French. (See *Ladies and
Gentlemen.*)

(2) There is a slight undercurrent against *all* Europeans
too. (*European* means white.) It is no stronger than anti-
Japanese feelings in Britain. No one can say that there
are strong anti-Japanese trends in Britain. Yet a Japanese
is a stranger, coming from distant shores. An alien is an
alien. And a *gaijin* is a *gaijin*.

(3) They look down upon the Koreans.

(4) They look down upon the Chinese. But they also look
up to the Chinese.

(5) People who are half-Japanese and half-American
(born in large numbers after the war) have a hard time. To
get good jobs is very, very difficult for them.

(6) When the American half was Negro, their lot was

much worse. Most of them left the country.

If you are half Negro, half Japanese and were born in Korea and brought up in China by European parents, do not emigrate to Japan.

Finally, there is a trace of anti-Japanese prejudice in Japan. The slight anti-Europeanism mentioned above combines with a slight European-mania. If you read Mr Kawasaki's book* you will see that he believes a love of Caucasians – as he calls us – to be Japan's main disease and that the Japanese are almost persecuted in their own country. I myself saw no evidence of actual persecution. Occasionally, it happened that in a crowd or in a restaurant, when I felt lost, I was politely helped while the Japanese were left on their own. But I needed help and they did not.

I did notice, however, that a few female Japanese pop-singers and television performers had had an operation to have their eyes straightened; I also saw a very few – two, to be precise – girls who had their beautiful black hair dyed blonde and red respectively. And I also saw many wax models in department stores with European instead of Japanese faces.

On the other hand there is no prejudice or intolerance vis-à-vis Japanese Americans – those Japanese who became Americans or were born in some of the Western States, and who no longer speak Japanese and feel – indeed *are* – Americans. I am glad to report that these people have improved their lot and their standing – and did so by sheer merit. During the war it was suspected by the Americans that they would form a fifth column. In fact, they proved themselves loyal, brave soldiers and this is remembered in the United States. There is not a shadow of resentment against them in Japan either. As one Japanese

* *Op. cit.*

novelist told me: 'They are Americans now. We want them to be *good* Americans.'

There are only two serious examples of racial prejudice.

(1) Koreans have a tough time. There are many of them in Japan – their country was colonised by the Japanese. It is extremely difficult, almost impossible, for them to become naturalised, yet one source of resentment against them is that they do not become Japanese subjects. It is very difficult for them to get good jobs; and impossible for them to be treated as equals.

As Koreans outwardly resemble the Japanese, many of them assume Japanese names and try to pass as natives.

A Japanese friend told me that a cousin of his wanted to marry a girl who on investigation turned out to be a Korean. The family opposed the marriage but the boy remained adamant so, in the end, the family gave in. A Japanese wedding is a splendid and costly ceremony: all the bridegroom's *and the bride's* close relations must be present. But to invite a Korean family was out of the question. So they hired about a hundred Japanese people who for a consideration – so many yen per hour – posed as the bride's family (her supposed father and mother got double fees). Today it is the Japanese family's darkest secret, a horrible skeleton in the cupboard, that they have a Korean in the family.

(2) The Etas. The Eta people were defeated in the Heike-Genji war and became the untouchables of Japan, below the four classes: the *samurai*, the farmers, the manufacturers and the merchants. (Note that professionals, artists, even priests had no class of their own.)

The Eta – now called the Buraku-Min – were despised. Their births and deaths were noted in separate registers. The situation was tolerable, however, as long as they stuck to their villages and kept strictly to themselves. But they, too, started moving to the large towns and there they met with grave difficulties. There is no *official* discrimination; the prejudice is purely social. Once, when I was travelling in a car with a Japanese friend, four of us, his passengers, suggested that we should stop at a roadside inn for a cold drink. He pretended not to hear us. Later I found out that the inn belonged to an Eta man, which explained why my friend, a broadminded and cosmopolitan chap in all other respects, could not bring himself to stop there.

The strongest resistance is to marriage. The special registers are no longer kept but the old volumes still exist and enquiry agents have mysterious access to them – although legally they should not. This private investigation is a nasty feature of Japanese life; as an angry Japanese friend remarked: 'The last vestige of the pre-war Thought Police.' If the girl turns out to be an Eta, the marriage is definitely off. Not even fake relatives would do in this case.

One interesting aspect: both Koreans and the Eta got into their inferior positions because they were defeated in war. They failed, so they must be inferior.

I was walking in the Roppongi district of Tokyo when I discovered a Jewish restaurant, run by a lady called Anne Dinken. It was, as I found out later, the only kosher restaurant in Tokyo, perhaps in Japan.

We were received and our orders were taken by a pretty Japanese girl called Reiko who spoke fluent English with a Yiddish accent. Then we witnessed an invasion by some Third Avenue and Bronx types, about six tall men, all looking like prize-fighters. Eventually Miss Dinken herself appeared, wearing a slightly garish skirt and stockings. I do not mean to be unkind, but Miss Dinken is a personality. Apart from being present in real life, she also looks down upon her guests from a poster. Coy and a little corpulent, she declares (on the poster): 'I am no geisha girl...' and goes on to recommend her *gefillte fisch,* salt beef and pastrami as well as the true Bronx ambience of her establishment. A man came in and said: 'Long time no see.' It turned out that he had left half an hour earlier. 'Missed me, honey?' – and he tried to kiss Miss Dinken, who pushed him away affectionately. Three women tried to persuade a fourth to join them, but she preferred the company of the virile prize-fighters.

'I don't blame you, honey,' one of the three shouted across the room.

'Thank you,' she replied venomously.

I asked Miss Dinken whether Japanese Jews ever visited her place.

'That's a myth, honey,' she told me. 'There are no Japanese Jews. Not a single one. Except the Emperor.'*

I stepped out of the restaurant, and was once again surrounded by the serious, ceremoniously bowing Japanese. That one step covered more than 10,000 miles.

When I talked to a friend about the existence of racial tension in Japan, he protested vehemently. He assured me that I was wrong and there was no trace of it.

'Take my own case, surely it is the best example,' he said. 'My family comes from China. Even my name is Chinese, it means silversmith. We came over to teach the Japanese our craft. There is no trace of prejudice against us; not a shadow of intolerance. We are accepted as if we were Japanese.'

'How long have you been here?'

'Eleven hundred years.'

---

* This was a little joke. The Emperor of Japan is not actually Jewish.

Kabuki Revisited

I shall start by recalling how Kabuki struck me when I first saw it:

A visit to Japan without seeing Kabuki is like a visit to Paris without seeing the Louvre. The Kabuki programme started at eleven o'clock in the morning with a seventh-century love-thriller involving Prince O'ama and Princess Nukada. There were three more plays in the morning; then we had an hour's break for lunch. In the afternoon it began all over again with a play called *Onna Shijin*. The hero of this was Gyo-Genki, a supremely beautiful woman and a great poetess, the daughter of Gyo-Bo, a 'madman in a house of pleasure'. Quite a promising start. The play itself lived up to our expectations.

Then came my own favourite, *The Earth Spider*. When the curtain rises we see the orchestra squatting at the back of the stage (as in all Kabuki plays), amid very impressive, beautiful scenery. We see a nobleman by the name of Minamoto Yorimutsu. He has fallen ill, and cannot understand what is wrong with him. People, by the way, do not speak in Kabuki plays: they chant in an artificial, monotonous, high-pitched voice; they also moan, mutter, groan, squeal, wail, whimper, whine, snivel and roar. This is a very ancient tradition and if you start watching Kabuki plays at the age of two, you may get used to it. If you start later, you wonder.

Yorimutsu is visited by Kocho, a ravishingly beautiful lady-in-waiting, who dances for the sick man. The dance does not cure him. Kocho is followed by another visitor in the guise of a travelling priest. But he is not a travelling priest at all, far from it: he is the Earth Spider. From his mask you can see immediately that he is not an attractive character. He walks in extremely slowly, roughly a quarter of a mile per hour. A number of other people – Yorimutsu's servants – sit, kneel, and squat about. Some people among the audience shriek with excitement. At last the visitor throws a spider at Yorimutsu who is, however, on the' alert; he jumps up, snatches his sword and slashes at the sham priest. The latter vanishes into thin air. 'Vanishing into thin air', is represented by his strolling away a little more slowly than he came.

All the members of the Yorimutsu household now gather together and decide that quick action must be taken. The Earth Spider must be sought out in his cave and destroyed. For about half an hour they chant and whine, 'Let's follow him! Let's run after him, we mustn't give him a chance to run away!' There is tremendous excitement, expressed by the fact that they all sit about quietly, almost motionless. They repeat: 'Let's hurry, let us gallop! We have not a moment to lose!' Whereupon they all remain seated.

The afternoon wears on. Suddenly Yorimutsu shouts: 'Aa ... !' (Emphasis on the second 'a'.) He stamps his foot twice. The chorus starts chanting again.

'Go, go and avenge yourself on the Earth Spider.'

Yorimutsu gives his answers in whispers: he informs his household that he is in a frantic rage and that they must hurry desperately, otherwise the monster might get away. One cannot be quick enough in such matters. Then he declares, 'Aa!' again and stamps his feet three times.

When I wake up three quarters of an hour later, the chase is at its height. Three men are moving about the stage to declare about a dozen times that everything depends on speed, otherwise the monster might have a chance to escape. Then the pace of the chase quickens; the three men – still motionless – become more emphatic on this point and sit down to debate it: 'Let us not spare ourselves! Who thinks of himself in such an hour as this? We have a sacred duty to perform.'

A number of pursuers now arrive, accompanied by a sort of gentle lullaby. They fully agree with the views of the Three. 'We cannot have a moment's rest until that curse, the Earth Spider is slain.' They sit down. A boy comes in moaning: 'Let us pursue him!' He performs a dance with two flags. After the dance the boy says: 'Let us not waste a single moment,' and dances another dance with seven fairies. The three original pursuers, still remarkably fresh although they have been squatting on the floor for so long, shout as the boy dances: 'Hurry, hurry! Not a moment is left!' The air is now so charged with urgency and tension that everyone sits down: the boy, the seven fairies and all.

Thirteen other people rush in on their knees. They lie down and kick their legs up into the air. They get up after a considerable time and dance first a doll-dance, then a puppet-dance and finally a Japanese polka. When this is over two men drag in a pedestal and leave it on the right side of the stage.

Someone starts knocking. The knocking goes on for twenty-three minutes. Another person chants: 'Oooooooh...' (emphasis on the last o) with guitar accompaniment for thirty-four minutes. Then he says: 'Oooooooh...' without the guitar for seventeen minutes. Then guitar without 'Oooooooh' for eighteen minutes.

The cave is pushed on with the monster inside. The pursuers reappear all dressed in yellow (I forgot to mention that they all went out during the 'Oooooooohs...' One of them makes a brief (nine minutes) chanting speech on the theme, 'We must not waste a minute otherwise the monster might get away'! They all squat, then get up, go out and reappear in green. This time they tell us about the frightful, hair-raising fate that awaits the Earth Spider.

They surround the cave and look at the monster but none of them sees him. The monster utters an awe-inspiring deafening howl: no one hears him. The pursuers say: 'We shall never find him. Our relentless pursuit was all in vain. The monster has managed to get away. Alas! All hope is lost.'

They dance round the cave. (They are in purple now.) Even the monster cannot bear to leave them in such deep despair any longer, so he comes out of the cave. At once they all sit down. A great deal of chanting ensues; the monster prepares for the final life-and-death struggle. But no one offers combat: in fact, no one moves. Suddenly the monster, the Earth Spider, collapses and dies. I think he has had a stroke. Boredom may have brought it on.

I have since felt slightly remorseful about these views. Was I too harsh? Did I lack understanding? Had I looked with arrogant, Western eyes at an ancient oriental tradition?

So I went to see Kabuki plays once again, as a reformed character, and found that, if anything, I had been too indulgent. Kabuki, of course, is an acquired taste but fewer and fewer young Japanese acquire it; they too look at it with arrogant Westernised eyes, or with condescending smiles, and regard it as modern British youth regard Trooping the Colour: a harmless but unimportant foible, remnant of a bygone age.

This time I saw it in the new National Theatre, an ingenious and attractive building, uniting the grace of old Japanese architecture with the requirements of a modern theatre. The auditorium was half empty.

The scenery of Kabuki is still beautiful; the movements

are often grotesque but just as often graceful; and the costumes are fabulous. But these are accessories and incidentals: the play's the thing – or should be. I watched it dejectedly and longed for the wit, speed and clarity of *The Earth Spider*. At least I could follow that play. This one had seven main and thirty-nine sub-plots. A wicked old man tried to seduce a beautiful young maiden. But everyone on stage looked like an ugly, middle-aged man and for a long time I could not make out which of them was the wicked seducer and which the beautiful young maiden.

In fact, they all *were* middle-aged men. There are no women in Kabuki, all the parts are played by men. An actor cannot just decide on the spur of the moment: 'Now I shall have a run in Kabuki.' One has to be trained for it for a lifetime and sons often follow in fathers' footsteps. It seems that before an actor is really good enough to play a leading part – that of a beautiful, innocent and young maiden – he must be a man of at least fifty-five.

Kabuki is going through a crisis and this crisis is typical of modern Japan. They try to accept Western ways; yet they also try to save as much of their ancient traditions as possible. This new production at the National Theatre was considerably de-traditionalised, modernised and Westernised. The orchestra was moved off the stage; there was much less moaning and whining – although more than enough remained. The whole performance was an odd mixture of traditional Kabuki, Edwardian music-hall fooling and Parisian *grand guignol* of the twenties. Of course it failed to come off; this modernisation is a self-defeating attempt. Some traditions stand up to modernisation, others don't. Often you may give new meaning to old ideas; you can frequently pour new wine into old bottles; but when the essence of the old tradition is simply old wine in old bottles, your task is more difficult. If you perform Kabuki it is better to follow the style of *The Earth Spider* and remain

defiantly antiquated, primitive and archaic. The old Kabuki had its devoted followers; the new seems to fall between an Eastern and a Western stool. One may wear a *kimono* or may go around dressed in blue jeans; but one cannot wear a *kimono* as if it were blue jeans. One cannot play the *hichiriki* as if it were the electric guitar.

Tempura Mutantur

On another subject, however, I am fully repentant: on Japanese food. I think it is delicious. It is not only the most original cuisine, really unlike anything to be found anywhere else – but also the most underrated.

At my first encounter with Japanese food I found it beautiful, like American food, but just as tasteless. Its smell was most appetising, its sound – you must eat noisily to show your appreciation – most melodious. In other words, Japanese food seemed to me pleasing to the eye, the nose and the ear. It was its taste, and its taste only, to which I objected.

Japanese cooking is related to Chinese as English is related to French. Both are overshadowed by their great, Continental neighbours. The dullness of English and Japanese food became so proverbial that people have failed to notice that both have improved beyond recognition in the last decade or so. On second thoughts, it is not my opinion that has changed: it is Japanese food. My advice to all visitors is: be adventurous and try the most exotic dishes and the chances are that you are in for an exciting, pleasing and completely novel kind of gastronomic experience. The taste of Japanese food has improved, and its beauty remains. Everything is served – usually even in the more modest places – with great aesthetic care. Every lunch is a food ceremony; every plate is an elaborate food-arrangement. They seem to employ not only cooks in their kitchens but also sculptors and plate-decorators.

The one Japanese dish which is well known all over the world is *sukiyaki*, and that is not Japanese at all: it is of Chinese origin. It is prepared from scores of ingredients and is cooked at the table on a little open flame, by the diners themselves. It has quite a few variations: *shabu-shabu* is one; the Genghis Khan barbecue – a variety of meats and delicious vegetables grilled at your table – is another. All this is great fun socially and quite delightful gastronomically but somewhat touristic and not the true food of Japan.

The true native food of Japan is fish. We abhor the idea of raw fish and exclaim: 'How barbaric!' Then we go out to eat oysters, roll-mops and *steak tartare*. Japanese raw fish – always fresh, beautifully cut in front of you, served with a piquant sauce and followed by heavenly pickles – is a great delicacy and I became a convert to both *sashimi* (plain raw fish) and *sushi* (slices of raw fish wrapped around small rice-balls). I even graduated to raw chicken; a thin slice of raw, marinated chicken is delicious indeed. The *yakitoriya* – the chicken restaurant – is another glory of Japan: you get chicken prepared in front of you in dozens of ways.

The fried fish, the *tempura*, is much nearer to our Western ideas. In a mediocre restaurant this can be a disappointment. You must choose your place carefully and you will find that there are endless, excellent varieties of *tempura*. As a great scholar, a student of both classical literature and Japanese cooking, so rightly remarked: *Tempura mutantur.*

A word about *sake*, their famous rice-wine. Some people say that they dislike *sake* and speak contemptuously about it, saying that they can drink any number of those tiny glasses without feeling any effect. But there is *sake* and *sake,* just as there is wine and wine: the varieties are many, the difference between good and bad *sake* is no smaller than the difference between third-rate retsina and a superb French claret. And as for taking any amount... well, some people carry their drink better than others. But remember: cold *sake* is (1) tasteless and (2) can be taken in large doses – although it's hardly worth taking it at all. Warm *sake* is incomparably better and knocks you out incomparably more quickly.

I love chopsticks, and don't mind eating sitting on the floor (as you have to if you choose a very Japanese restaurant, otherwise you sit on chairs). I must admit that squatting is an acquired skill and I am less than a beginner. I am normally rather clumsy with my hands but I have a natural, native skill with chopsticks. I can use them with the ease and assurance of an elderly *samurai.*

Sitting on the floor eating small bits of food and lumps of rice with chopsticks cured me of one of my little failings. Never, not once, did I drop a greasy bit of food on the lapel of my jacket or on my tie. I always dropped it on my trousers.

You can carry this passion of going Japanese a little too far. Once, with a number of English residents in Tokyo, we went to a very Japanese Japanese restaurant in a hidden corner of popular Asakusa – off the beaten track where few tourists turn up. We were led up to one of those small, special rooms where the meals are served and on the way up one of my companions discovered one of his friends – another Englishman – having dinner, squatting on the floor with apparent ease.

'I envy you,' he said. 'The one thing I cannot learn is this squatting.'

'Quite easy, really,' the other replied, a shade patronisingly, I thought.

We proceeded to the neighbouring room, ate our dinner and would have forgotten about him but for his unexpected reappearance. He had wanted to straighten his tired legs – squatting was easy but not that easy – had lost his balance, rolled over, fallen against the thin paper-wall, burst through it and ended up – with proper English apologies – in my soup.

A Crypto-Matriarchy

'If you want to be a Japanese, be a man.' This is the advice most superficial observers would give you. But it is not followed by about half of Japan's population and they know what they are doing. 'It's a man's country,' the short-term visitor would add. The long-term visitor would not be quite so sure.

Most Japanese live a double life: a Western one in the office and in public and a Japanese one at home. Most of them wear Western dress for work and *kimono* or *yukata* – the dressing-gown version of the *kimono* – in the house. This may not be only the result of devotion to tradition, but also of good sense. I have little Japanese blood in my veins but I got into the *yukata*-habit soon enough: it's pleasant, comfortable and cool. Whatever the reasons and motives, once people wear Japanese dress they behave in a Japanese manner. Even I did. Dress maketh the man. I have noticed that some of my close friends behave like eighteenth century courtiers when they put on tails, like Edwardian clubmen when wearing dinner-jackets and like itinerant students – even if well over fifty – as soon as they don blue jeans on Greek islands.

In Japan, between the two lives of the people there is the *shoe*. I believe that the shoe-barrier is an important dividing line. I am not speaking simply of the rule that you take your shoes off when entering a Japanese house – this is purely physical. My point is that the *psychology of the shoe* has not been properly explored. When a Western resident in Japan starts expatiating on the cleanliness and sensibleness of the Japanese habit of not wearing shoes inside the house, then he has caught the oriental bug and has fallen for Japan in a big way; when a Japanese suddenly declares: 'To hell with it! I am tired of taking my shoes off all the time. I don't do it in the office, why should I do it at home . . .' then he is truly Westernised. (He will, nevertheless, have to go on taking his shoes off at home. Japanese floor coverings – the famous *tatami* – are not made for shoes.)

The point I am driving at is this: the consequences of this double life are seemingly disastrous for the women. In the home they are treated as they were in the old days, they have to obey their lords and masters, and on top of that they are totally excluded from their husbands' Western life, the often gay and eventful social life which follows office hours.

In many households, when the master comes home the wife bows; if they walk together in the streets of their neighbourhood, the wife walks behind her husband; if, home again, the husband sits down, he will not dream of getting up to get a newspaper: he will snap his fingers and his wife will fetch it for him; if the family has only one bath tub, there is no question as to who should have first bath.

But all this is changing in various ways and for diverse reasons. More and more women go out to work. More and more women – even in the remotest country places – watch television (nearly a hundred per cent of the people have the box and see a different way of life every day). Many of them, therefore, are now refusing to remain their husbands' – or fathers' – obedient and obsequious servants. There has not been a violent revolution: there has been – and it is continuing – a slow change of attitudes.

Younger women in growing numbers – but still in a minority – refuse to be told by their parents whom they are to marry; and young men, too, silently refuse to accept their parents' choice. Today, as likely as not, they will obey their firm's orders instead: one group replaces the other. The firm is a reactionary influence but not quite so reactionary as the family, which is not only a closed, incestuous entity, not only one of the most conservative of forces, but also, and obviously, the paradigm of the hereditary principle.

The more spirited and adventurous women revolt more or less openly – and many of them do not even have to revolt because their husbands dislike the old feudal ways as much as they do. But, even today, the revolutionaries are the exception. People, on the whole, do not really want freedom: indeed, they run away from it. Freedom means responsibility – one of the most terrifying things in the world, hence the success of religions, of the Communist Parties and of the various Hitlers of the various ages. Usually it is a few outstanding, admirable individuals who force freedom on an unwilling mob, which is always ready to pay lip-service to the idea but does not want it in practice. British and American suffragettes met as much opposition from women as from men; the majority of Swiss women still do not want the vote (Japanese women, as I have said before, have it); and there are many Negroes who oppose all Civil Rights movements.

Yet Japanese women have another, more powerful motive for the fight than the desire for freedom.

Household work in Japan used to be heavier than in Europe and much heavier than in the United States. It is true that there is less furniture in the house, but putting away the heavy mats every morning and dragging them out every evening is heavier work than making the bed in our way. Cooking, too, means an enormous amount of fiddling work in antiquated kitchens, and the innumerable tiny dishes do not make washing up any easier. (Any husband would, of course, roar with laughter at the mere idea that he might help.) Shopping is easier because everything is sent home free of charge. But the poorer woman's life used to be drudgery, and the richer woman's complete boredom. The latter had servants and all Japanese women – rich and poor – are exempt from one duty: entertaining at home. Women are often alone during long evenings while their husbands are working hard for promotion in first class restaurants, night-clubs and geisha-houses, often until the early hours of the morning, poor fellows.

Nowadays, however, more and more women are relieved from the drudgery. Husbands, perhaps with slightly uneasy consciences, are quite happy to buy washing machines, washing-up machines and all sorts of new gadgets, not realising that their generosity, instead of appeasing their wives, turns them into rebels. Drudgery they used to accept as their inevitable lot; increased boredom they refuse to put up with. They suffer intensely from it, and although the innumerable channels of Japanese television may alleviate it, they cannot eliminate it. A noble desire for freedom will move only a few; a desire to escape boredom is creating a mass movement.

The brave ones rebel, the spirited ones want a change, but the truly cunning ones know that their situation is not half as bad as it seems. It is true that the man gets all the bows and enjoys many outward signs of respect, but he is like a constitutional monarch: he walks on red carpets all his life, enjoys the trimmings of power but has very little of the substance. He reigns, perhaps, but he does not rule. It is the little, oppressed, obsequious female who wields the real power. As a Japanese friend told me ruefully: 'I'll tell you a secret: Japan is, in fact, a matriarchy. Worse than the United States.'

That poor little oppressed women in the background holds the reins and is, very frequently, a formidable personality. It is she who makes all the decisions concerning the household and the house, about the children's education, about the children's marriages (as far as they will listen) and – most important of all – she is the family treasurer; her fingers are on the purse strings and thus on the levers of real power.

The extent of female power is borne out by the birth of a new industry, unique to Japan. It is the false pay-packet industry. Millions of Japanese men – the great majority of them – have no access to the expense accounts racket and they would like to have a little more money for themselves. But they have strict orders from their poor, oppressed wives to bring their pay-packets home unopened and they would not dare to disobey. That's where the new industry comes in. Pay-packets are printed and supplied to order, showing the required, smaller sums; replicas of the company's bags, typography, pay slips, etc. A man can open his real pay-packet, take out a few thousand yen for his own private use and still deliver a properly sealed and seemingly unopened pay-packet to the higher authority.

If this goes on for long the oppressive and lordly Japanese male will have to strike a blow for his emancipation and start an *Equal Rights for Men* movement.

Something like it is already in the air. Why should certain occupations be closed to men? I have not heard of male geishas yet but male hostesses – well, hosts, if I may coin a word – have made their first appearance.

A charming Irish lady who works as a governess for an English family in Tokyo told me about her experience of this. She went into a newly opened café and ordered a cold drink. A pleasant, good-looking, smartly dressed, well-spoken young man approached her and asked for permission to sit at her table. Having received permission, he sat down, ordered a lemonade for himself, and proceeded to chat to her most amusingly for about twenty minutes. The lady – pretty and charming but no longer in her twenties – felt very pleased with her success: the young man was at least ten years younger than she. She stood up and said goodbye to her companion.

'Thank you very much,' she said warmly.

'What do you mean, "thank you very much"?' asked the young man, painfully surprised. 'You will be charged for my drink and you owe me 300 yen.'

A footnote to this remarkable development. Mr Michikhiro Kono, the manager of Tokyo's latest and biggest host-club, the Night Miyamasu, told a reporter of the *Asahi Evening News* that his night-club used to be a conventional one with hostesses instead of 'social partners' – as he preferred to call his young men – but the club proved to be more profitable after the changeover. He added that more than six hundred and twenty men applied when the night-club advertised jobs for men between eighteen and thirty-five, offering a monthly salary of Y 200,000 (£ 235 or $560). As work starts at 5.30 p.m. the men could take this employment as a second job. Applicants included employees of reputable trading firms, high-school teachers and former Japanese Self-Defence Force personnel. Ten per cent of them were married men. One of the applicants brought written permission from his wife.

The Geisha

In all disputes and discussions the first rule is: clarify your terms. This is important in philosophy – linguistic or otherwise – in politics, in political science and in law. Whole books, indeed whole libraries, have been written on the interpretation of an 'and' or an 'a' in a statute or an international treaty. Clear definition of terms is important in all fields, but in none more so than that concerned with geishas.

Westerners of both sexes are often under the impression that the geisha girl is a superior kind of prostitute. But Western husbands on their return to Manchester, Los Angeles or Melbourne are at pains to explain to their wives that they are not: nothing could be farther from the truth, they say with a slightly nervous laugh. Geishas are cultured young ladies with exquisite manners, they are dancers, singers and entertainers of great talent, and it is not on their skill in the art of love but on their skill in repartee that their reputation rests.

The truth – at least *one* truth, I shall come to the other presently – is that the geisha girl is a cultured and highly trained young prostitute with a gift for repartee.

It is equally true, nevertheless, that while geishas can be bought for the night (it is a matter of price and a very high price at that), a geisha-party, much more often than not, means only supper, drinking *sake,* watching dancing and listening to singing and gay conversation (full of repartee). *Mamasan* – the wise and all powerful supervisor and mentor of the girls (it would be horribly rude to call her the brothel-keeper) – is not surprised if someone wishes to linger late in one of the tiny little houses where the parties take place but, as a rule, after midnight the guests return to their family hearths.

A young German who had been living in Tokyo for about four years and was well on the way to making a business career for himself, talked to me on this subject.

'I am speaking to you man to man,' he said. 'Please don't give me away, it would make me look ridiculous. I should lose face and that's fatal here. Promise?'

I promised.

He looked around cautiously and then he went on.

'I love my wife. She is a Japanese girl. I have never been unfaithful to her and do not intend to be. All the same, I have to spend at least three nights a week in brothels. Very well, call them geisha-houses. I slip away at midnight, and so do most of my Japanese business friends. It's not so bad when you can slip out. But I can't get out of going to the parties. How would you like to go to brothels three times a week?'

I found this question unnecessarily personal and left it unanswered.

'My wife doesn't suspect me of being faithful to her,' he went on. 'That's my shady secret. She would think rather poorly of me if she found out. You won't talk? You promised . . .'

I told him not to worry. I might write about him in my book but apart from that I wouldn't breathe a word.

'The other day I thought I had tricked three Japanese,' he said with a wide grin. 'I produced the contracts from my desk out of the blue and handed them a pen. All this was in my office, mind you. They were so taken aback

and confused that they signed. After they'd gone, I felt
pretty elated. "No geishas for me tonight," I thought antici-
pating the pleasures of a geisha-less evening. But I laughed
too soon. That evening, the three Japanese gentlemen, all
smiles and bows, reappeared in my office. They did not
explain why they had come. They didn't need to. Off we
went to the bro ... I mean to one of those houses of traditional geisha entertainment.'

The Americans have established another great 'first', fore-
stalling all other nations. The achievement is less famous
than their landing on the moon but not much less remarkable. They have the first American geisha in Tokyo.

This American lady wears a beautiful *kimono* and her
blonde hair is made up in a high coiffure, in true geisha-
style. She sings Japanese songs and accompanies herself on
the guitar; when she runs out of Japanese songs, a few saucy
American songs help out. Her repartee is rumoured to be a
shade less *raffiné* than that of her Japanese counterparts
but it is still lightning quick. Americans living in Tokyo
would not touch her with a barge-pole; they say – most
unfairly – that she is just a prostitute with a gimmick.
Americans – and other white people – remain faithful to
Japanese geishas. But Japanese businessmen flock to her
and used to queue up in front of her bedroom door: the
attraction of a blonde American woman proved irresistible
for many. I say 'used to' queue up – not because her attraction has waned but she has been doing a roaring trade and
has grown rich; nowadays she can pick and choose her
clients. All the same, her enemies maintain that her business
is controlled by her pimp whom she calls *Papasan*.

But, as I remarked earlier, clarification of terms is most
necessary. These girls whom I have just described do indeed
call themselves geishas nowadays; other people call them

geishas too. But this is an abuse of the term. Demand for geishas and for their services became so great that these girls – not really properly trained – made the best of a sellers' market. Admirers of the real geishas refer to them, most contemptuously, as pillow-geishas, girls who can be hired for the night.

The true geisha is a bird of very different plumage. Not that she is not a prostitute: she is. But she is the finest, most cultured and most treasured prostitute one can find anywhere; and the only prostitute who is genuinely respected, and rightly so.

When a geisha reaches the end of her very long and thorough training in the art of conversation, repartee, singing, dancing, playing the guitar, tea-ceremony, flower arrangement, etc. (and more on the Education of Geishas in the chapter on Kyoto, which is the greatest university-town for geishas, their Cambridge or Harvard) she will be, more likely than not, a virgin. She will be about twenty or twenty-one years old and ready for her first patron. *Mama-san* of the tea-house will know the girl well and appreciate her real value; she will also know the market. The girl may be chosen by a would-be patron and then her consent will be asked for. She is absolutely free to say no. If she says yes, she will move into the house her patron buys for her. The house is hers and remains hers whatever happens.

'Would the patron's wife know?' I asked a very knowledgeable gentleman who was an expert on the subject. He shrugged his shoulders.

'Sometimes she knows and approves: to have a geisha confers status. Sometimes she knows and disapproves but this makes very little difference. A woman can divorce a man in Japan but his adultery is not one of the reasons for divorce. Sometimes she prefers not to know – and then she doesn't.'

The details of the actual financial arrangement are always most discreetly handled and never revealed to anyone. As a rule the patron simply pays all the geisha's bills and, when the original arrangement is made, he also pays a handsome commission to *Mamasan*.

The association between the geisha and her first patron is often lifelong. She is, in fact, a second wife, in some cases more faithful, more loyal and more of a real partner than the first. Marriage in many cases is nothing more than legalised prostitution; the geisha-patron relationship, on the other hand, is often a non-legalised marriage. Sometimes the association lasts for a few years only and the geisha is as free to terminate it as her patron. Even if she does so the house remains hers. The geishas are proud girls, tend to be faithful to their patrons and few have more than two or three patrons during a lifetime. Their houses are usually beautiful and elegant and they are, I repeat, truly respected members of society; they are also a dying-out species.

Having found their patrons, they go on working as geishas, i.e. they go out to entertain at parties, to sing and dance for other men, but they are strictly monogamous – if this be the right word – and remain faithful to their patrons. One cannot and one does not make an indecent offer to a proper geisha-girl any more than one does to one's friend's wife.

Which means that occasionally one does. And it also means – as geishas are only virtuous human beings, not angels – that such offers are occasionally accepted. The girl may then bid farewell to her patron and accept a new one; or she may carry on a secret love-affair with the choice of her heart, on the side.

'Does the patron, as a rule, find out?' I asked.

'Sometimes he does, sometimes he doesn't,' my philosophical friend replied. 'Sometimes he pretends not to know, sometimes not to care, and in some cases he makes a fuss and breaks off the relationship. He behaves foolishly or wisely, as other husbands behave the world over. This is a marriage after all. In the West the average male has two wives – consecutively, one after the other; in Japan – in the class which can afford geishas at all – he has two wives simultaneously. That's the only difference. The superiority of one system over the other is open to debate.'

Places

Tokyo

Many Japanese will tell you that Tokyo is an ugly city. You must not disagree with them because that would be discourteous; you must not agree with them either, because that would be even more discourteous. You say: 'Beauty is in the eye of the beholder,' or quote Wilde or Kant on beauty in general. But whatever you may say and whomever you may quote, Tokyo remains an ugly city. There are hardly any beautiful or even good buildings (one I liked, Frank Lloyd Wright's old Imperial Hotel, was pulled down between my two visits); there are very few parks; there are no mountains or even hills inside or outside the city; there is no green belt; there are few monuments worth looking at; the air pollution is terrifying; the perpetual noise deafening; the traffic murderous. Go to Rio de Janeiro, Hong Kong or Istanbul if you want to admire natural beauty in a city, or if you want to see buildings go to Paris, Rome or Venice.

Some people compare Tokyo's vastness to that of London. The two towns are very different and even their vastness cannot be compared: London is a galaxy of countless villages, Tokyo is an overgrown small town. Tokyo reminds you, perhaps, of Los Angeles, a dreary conglomeration of houses without a real centre but, once again, with a great difference. Los Angeles has a rich population who live in excellent, spacious houses; Tokyo's population is growing richer and richer, but housing conditions are appalling.

Foreigners often complain that their Japanese friends never invite them to their houses. They cannot. Quite well-to-do people live in conditions of such overcrowding that no English or Swedish labourer would put up with it for a day. In London the average living space a person occupies is 9.2 square metres, in New York 11.9 square metres; in Tokyo only 0.4 square metres. In other words, the average inhabitant of Tokyo lives in an imaginary room the dimensions of which are eight inches by eight inches. But the trouble is not only lack of space. Forty-seven per cent of the houses should be condemned for one reason or another. Only one quarter of them have proper drainage, and sanitary conditions – to use the euphemism of the century – are old-fashioned. The situation in the country is worse. Rents are exorbitant. To pay £5,000 or £6,000 a year for a really good though not vast flat in Tokyo is not unusual, and a reasonable room (called a bed-sitter) costs Y 10,000 (£12 or $50) a week.

Little wonder Japanese do not want to invite people to their places. The idea has been generally accepted that the proper place for entertainment is a luxurious restaurant, and that it would even be discourteous to invite a friend to one's humble home.

Housing conditions do not improve fast enough. Too many office blocks are being built and not enough dwelling houses; and also too many garages. A Japanese cannot obtain a licence to buy a car until he can prove that he has somewhere to put it off the street. So cars are often housed before people.

Having said all this, I must add a word of qualification. While housing conditions are bad, often shocking, many lucky people live very comfortably. And, much more important, do not suppose that even the poorer – even the poorest – Japanese homes are places of degrading squalor. With their inborn tidiness and exquisite aesthetic sense, they make the best of their opportunities. Furniture is sparse even in the richest Japanese house – Japanese houses do not *need* furniture – and it is amazing what a difference a little taste, a little care and love and a few freshly cut and decoratively arranged flowers can make. All the flats or houses I saw were small; all were tidy, attractive and dainty. Even the poorest and most modest place had a charm and dignity of its own.

Due to the lack of space people go out of their homes whenever possible. This habit adds yet another injustice to the position of women. The old-fashioned Japanese man associates glamour, happiness and the beauties of life with being away from his home; and associates poverty, drabness and worries with his wife.

There are 80,000 bars in Tokyo alone for people to escape to; one bar for every hundred and fifty persons, including babies, children, the sick and aged.

Hotels are very good. The rooms are lovely, often spacious, and equipped with every kind of modern gadget, bells, telephone, radio and television. Sheets are changed daily and a clean *yukata* – dressing-gown, as no doubt the reader remembers – is also provided every day. One also gets, every day, a new toothbrush and toothpaste, and a brand new little razor with a new blade. The only trouble with Tokyo's excellent hotels is that there are not enough of them. I arrived there about three weeks before I'd planned to – in other words, naïvely and hopefully, without a hotel reservation. But for my airline, Lufthansa, I would have slept under a tree in one of Tokyo's few parks.

I feel the least I can do to make up for the trials and tribulations I caused to Lufthansa is to pay a short tribute to them here. That they are an excellent airline as far as *flying* is concerned – perhaps a not altogether unimportant consideration – goes without saying. The usual advertised amenities are all there (which is not always the case with all famous airlines). But their service started long before take-off and went on long after landing. They regarded me as their 'charge' – I *was* their charge, I suppose – and they looked after me with avuncular affection. Not having finished my work in time at one place, or having finished it earlier than I expected at another, I had to change my bookings quite frequently, upsetting weeks of careful planning. I arrived in Tokyo – Tokyo! – without a hotel reservation. I had all my mail sent to their various offices and letters often had to be forwarded to new destinations. I had to plan train and car journeys to, and needed information about, towns to which they did not even fly. And finally they found me a delightful Greek island and a hotel room at the height of the season, where I could settle down and write this book. Courteous, smiling officials were always at my disposal throughout all this, acting as if they were pleased to see me turn up once again, with yet another impossible request. I think of them not only with gratitude but with almost filial piety.

I have spoken candidly about Tokyo's ugliness and shortcomings. But there is a reverse side to the coin.

Old Tokyo is slowly disappearing. The town has suffered much from earthquakes and aerial bombardment, and many houses have been pulled down. New, large office blocks go up in place of the small houses, and the sky-line of Tokyo changes rapidly. Because of the fear of earthquakes – Tokyo has about twenty a day, most of them unnoticed except by seismographs – the erection of high buildings used to be forbidden; now new ways of using steel, and the compulsory building of two, three or four basement floors, has made tall blocks possible. The result of the new office-block or skyscraper mania is that Tokyo is losing its peculiar, individual ugliness and acquiring an international, customary ugliness which we meet all over the world and to which we are becoming resigned.

But not all is ugliness in Tokyo. There *are* a few – I repeat, a few – good buildings and impressive temples and shrines; there are a few – and I must repeat again, a few – parks worth visiting. And the overcrowding, the lack of space, has one advantage, pleasing at least to the eye. Everything has to be small in Tokyo: houses, rooms, shops – even, one feels, people, to fit into the small houses. Long side-streets consist of tiny houses only, and this often creates a toy-like, unreal yet engaging quality, with small women tip-toeing along in their *kimonos* and equally small men sitting, motionless, inside their tiny shops.

Tokyo at night is a very different place from Tokyo in daytime. After the offices have closed and the commuters have left town, Tokyo puts on a new face. Millions of neon-signs are switched on and nowhere in the world are they more attractive, more bewitching, more maddeningly fast-moving than here. The cafés, bars and night-clubs, *sushi*-places, *yakitoriya*, Chinese restaurants and Korean barbecues, theatres, cinemas, cineramas, strip-tease joints and many other establishments open their doors and a new type of leisurely, pleasure-seeking or simply admiring awe-struck crowd mills around the Ginza and other entertainment districts. This wild, high and mondaine night-life goes on and on and on – until 10.30 at night. Then people jump into taxis and drive home at breathtaking speed, facing a thousand deaths. Some night-clubs stay open till much later, but they are exceptions. By 11 p.m. all the gaiety and sin is over (earlier on Sundays); even the naughty girls – most of them – are home and in bed, alone.

A town is not its buildings alone; it is its atmosphere, its ambience, its feel, its pleasures, its sadness, its madness, its disappointments and above all its people. Tokyo may lack architectural beauty but it has character and excitement; it is alive. I found it a mysterious and lovable city.

Kyoto

'If Tokyo is ugly, Kyoto is beautiful,' many people will tell you. This statement, put in this way, is not true. Tokyo *is* ugly but only with reservations; and the same goes for Kyoto's beauty. To be sure, Kyoto is full of impressive temples, gardens and shrines of immortal, breath-taking beauty, grace and majesty; you can see great, impressively – sometimes almost oppressively – powerful works of art; and the surrounding mountains are lush and enchanting yet serene; inviting yet forbidding. You can find more beauty, man-made and natural, in Kyoto than anywhere else in Japan, but the city itself, with its three million people, its mad traffic, its heat and noise, cannot be called beautiful; in a way – as we shall see – it is uglier than most Japanese cities.

Kyoto used to be called Heiankyo in the old days; it became the capital of Japan in 794 and remained capital for well over a millenium. It is quieter, more reserved, more formal in manners, better dressed and more elegant than busy, modern, industrial Tokyo and is well aware of its real or imaginary distinction. There is a nostalgic and pathetic, slightly comic yet endearing, dignity in all former capitals, from Winchester to Toledo, from Berlin to Kyoto – rather similar to the hurt feelings of grandeur you find in dispossessed aristocrats. They (both the ex-capitals and the dispossessed aristocrats) are deeply offended because times have changed. They are right in maintaining that the old days – their own days of greatness – were less noisy and vulgar than modern times; yet one knows that the real virtue of these old times is that *they* were grand and important then while today they are nobodies – or, at best, only second-rate. They are sulky and self-conscious but also gentle, more quiet, more distinguished, more respectable than their *parvenu* rivals. All that is left to them is a feeling of superiority and a great deal of nostalgia for bygone days. Kyoto – even today more of an ex-capital than a busy tourist-centre – looks down upon the world. Only nearby Nara can get the better of it. Nara can look down upon Kyoto: it *ceased* to be Japan's capital in 794.

In Kyoto, particularly in the Gion district, you go back in time. Fifty years? Or a hundred? Kyoto, being full of art treasures, is the only great city of Japan which escaped bombing in the last war and thus preserved its ancient charm but also its ancient squalor. It is because of this that Kyoto is not only incomparably more beautiful than most Japanese cities, but also uglier.

But it is pleasant to wander back in time. You see rows of small houses, tiny inns, old-fashioned restaurants piled one upon another. Romantic old passages invite you; dark and graceful arcades beckon to you; tiny paper houses with infinitesimal rooms open up their secrets to you and you see that eight or ten people live in one room with the cleanliness and tidiness common to all Japanese. You pass dustbins, scores of dustbins, put out for collection, all bright red and blue and purple, polished and shining more brightly than Swiss door-handles. You move around in the narrow, dark passages. You, incorrigible occidental, expect a few juvenile delinquents with coshes to leap out from the shadows demanding money – but all you meet is the shy but inquisitive look on friendly, good-natured faces. There are miniature shrines everywhere in this city of a thousand temples. You look into the houses through the curtain-doors only half drawn and see a very old woman crouching there, gazing into the infinite distance with an empty look, or a young woman busily preparing pickles for her husband who, close beside her, deep in thought, is eating rice from a bowl. The Gion itself, Kyoto's Ginza, is gay, florid, bustling and noisy. This apparent den of iniquity closes down at 9.30. You long for the reckless gaiety of Tokyo's Ginza where they keep open till as late as 10.30. Though to be precise: here, in Kyoto, it is only the cafés, restaurants, bars and semi-night-clubs which close at 9.30; the shops keep open till 10.30. You cannot get a drink, not even a lemonade after ten; but you can buy a pressure cooker or a pair of shoes.

After a few minutes in Kyoto's Gion district you notice exquisitely dressed and elaborately made up young ladies walking along the streets and jumping into waiting taxis or private cars. They wear ceremonial *kimonos* made of brocade and silk, their artistically arranged, towering hair-styles add a foot to their height and their faces are painted white like porcelain. They are the *maiko* girls, the student geishas, almost the only students in Japan who are not on strike. (They soon will be.) When you catch sight of them in the streets for a fleeting moment, what they are doing is rushing from one party to another.

'They are all virgins,' your friends and guides will inevitably assure you. You smile cynically and say to yourself: 'Of course. Because as soon as they cease to be virgins, no doubt, they inform everyone of the fact!' But you are wrong and your guide is right: the girls *are* virgins. Firstly, they have no opportunity, living under strict supervision as they do, to lose their virginity; and secondly, they do not even want to. They are all between the ages of sixteen and twenty-two. At the age of twenty-two they will become fully-fledged geishas and go to live with their patrons who will insist upon their virgin state: virginity is a precious and saleable commodity; it is true, of course, that it can be bought and remade to measure, but it is simpler and cheaper to keep the original article.

The *maiko* girls will go out and entertain people, sing and dance to them, do everything a geisha does, but they will not yet have a patron. The *maiko* starts her general training for becoming a geisha at the age of six; she will go on to intensified and more specialised training from sixteen to twenty-two, another six years – which makes it sixteen years altogether. What the hell do they learn during all this time? you wonder. The art of flower arranging with its three main styles, *seika, moribana* and *nageire,* as well as complicated rules for special occasions, is not exactly simple but – make a generous allowance – three years should be sufficient to learn it all; 'tea-ism', as the art of the tea-ceremony is called, is not much less complicated, but surely during the same three years one could grasp it? The girls learn to dance but their dances consist of tiny timid steps to left and right, backwards and forwards, and even I – not a born dancer – could learn this in three days. And they cannot really play the guitar. Their conversation and their repartee may be devastating, although I doubt it; but all these years of training are not sufficient to teach them one single word of any foreign language. You hate to seem uncharitable and ungallant, but you keep on wondering: how is it that a physician can qualify in six years but a whore – even if she is the most accomplished and delightful whore in the world – needs sixteen?

For getting rid of money and impressing on your foreign or Japanese friends that 'I can afford it', the *maiko* girl system is unbeatable. An hour and a half in the company of two *maiko* girls, with a few drinks but without a morsel of food, costs Y 30,000 (£35 or $85). That's the bare minimum and to spend no more would look rather stingy, and this is only the beginning of an evening's entertainment. For this sum you are entertained by two dolls painted white, who cannot play the guitar properly, cannot dance and with whom you cannot exchange one single word. The fully qualified geishas cost twice as much; and as a Japanese friend – a great authority on the subject – remarked, are twice as boring.

This boredom is a grave threat to the whole industry. *Maiko* girls are bored stiff themselves, and few young girls are prepared to become *maikos*. That's where the strike threatens. In the old days starving fathers had to sell their young daughters to tea-houses to get a few yen and in the hope that the girls would have a better life than they would in their own miserable home. Those days, however, have passed: Japan is one of the most prosperous countries of the world and no one needs to sell his daughter. So it is mostly daughters of tea-house owners and daughters of geishas who are persuaded – not without difficulty – to become *maikos* and to keep up the family tradition and – more important – the family business. And once the girls have been persuaded to take the plunge, they have to work like studious schoolgirls and live like nuns.

The would-be patrons also show signs of being bored with the whole system. As girls of their own class become more emancipated, they become more and more accessible, and they are better company than the *maikos* and geishas.

So the system is slowly withering away, being bored out of existence.

No *maiko* girl can become a geisha before she is twenty-two. But how long can she remain a geisha? There is no age-limit. It is like acting Romeo or a beautiful and bashful maiden in Kabuki: you must reach a certain age before you can do it properly. An English friend, who had been a frequent guest at geisha parties for years, told me that he had never met a geisha worth listening to under the age of forty.

The most popular geisha of Kyoto – the city of *maiko* girls, all , under twenty-two – is a lady in her middle seventies. She is adored, much in demand and commands exorbitant fees. She had about five different patrons in her younger days and has none today; but she is witty, well-read, quick on the uptake and has an inexhaustible repertoire of naughty songs – new and old – which she sings with gusto and with an attractive twinkle in her eye.

'Some of Kyoto's ruins may be older but none is more attractive,' remarked my English friend of this lady.

I don't think he was right.

Some of the temples, art treasures and gardens are fabulous. My favourite – not for its beauty but as a place of interest – is the Nijo Castle in Nikomura Palace. It has a special waiting room for feudal lords, another one for non-hereditary feudal lords, then one for the sons of feudal lords, one for the sons of non-hereditary feudal lords, one for the brothers-in-law of non-hereditary feudal lords and so on. Then we have the *shogun's* audience chambers for feudal lords, for non-hereditary feudal lords and so on, down to the audience chamber for the brothers-in-law of non-hereditary feudal lords. The *shogun's* living quarters struck me as particularly splendid and luxurious, but it was explained that they were simple and austere. Because, I was told, he – the first *shogun* who had this palace built – was a simple and austere man. He had one single bedroom for himself and then only a few more for his concubines. He always left his wife in Tokyo – Edo – when he came down here but he was always regarded as an ascetic man, a man of admirable self-restraint, because at no given time did he have more than two hundred concubines.

The other rooms had lovely, poetic names. Willow Room

(where Feudal Lords were identified); Rosy Dawn Room (where they were searched); Hyacinth Room (where they were tortured) and, I believe, the Chamber of Heavenly Pleasure where they were executed.

They also have the Nightingale Floor in the palace. It has got this romantic name because when you walk on it, it gives out a whispering sound, sad and rueful, like a nightingale hopelessly in love. The reason for this romantic arrangement is not a love of nightingales but a desire to detect people who came stealing along the corridors, wanting to assassinate the *shogun*.

But where my friend went really wrong in his comparison between the elderly geisha and Kyoto's ruins was in saying that some of the ruins might be older than she. My suspicion is that none of them is. Not because that charming and illustrious lady is so old – what is three score years and ten, or say fifteen, nowadays? – but because all Kyoto's ruins are so incredibly young.

Wherever you go, you read descriptions of old temples and monuments which go like this:

'Built in the eighth century. Burnt down and completely rebuilt in 893, 1217, 1526, 1718 and 1933. The present structure of this lovely eighth century Temple was erected in 1965.'

Is this Japan all over again? The land of the most up-to-date, up-to-the-minute, antiquity; the land of brand-new ancientness?

Osaka

Osaka is the third city of Japan the foreign tourist is likely to visit, particularly if he is of indomitable spirit and prepared to face Expo 70.

There is the same, inevitable rivalry between Osaka and Tokyo as between many first and second cities: between Rio de Janeiro and São Paulo, between Sydney and Melbourne, between Rome and Florence, between Stockholm and Gothenburg. As in the case of the Brazilian and the Swedish towns mentioned, one is the real, the other the commercial capital of the country. (I have heard of Brazilia, of course; but it is not yet the real capital of Brazil.) Osaka used to be called the Manchester of Japan, a title of which – I was told – it used to be extremely proud.

'Osaka is a village,' people in Tokyo will tell you.

'There are far too many people in Tokyo,' your Osaka friends will remark.

'Well, Osaka is not really a village,' you will reply, to which the Osaka-ites will add. 'Three million people. Just right.' (A few weeks later I heard the same remark about the small Austrian town, Kufstein. 'It has 12,000 people. Just right.' Three million is just right; twelve thousand is just right.)

Osaka is a big, industrial, commercial and banking city, with 'no culture' as Tokyo people are fond of repeating and

Osaka people are quite ready to agree; they take it almost as a compliment. They prefer cash to symphony orchestras. It is one of the oldest Japanese jokes (of which there aren't many) that Osaka people spend all their money on food, Kyoto people on clothes and Tokyo people on politics. (As I have pointed out earlier, more money seems to be made on politics than spent on it, but I reproduce the quip as I heard it.) It is another joke that people in Osaka do not greet one another with the customary 'Good morning' or 'Good day', but with the question: 'How's business?' To which the expected answer is the Japanese equivalent of 'So-so'.

When I visited Osaka it was burning with Expo-fever. Urban motorways, highways and hotels had been built; the Expo site buzzed with feverish activity. Special police were being trained to help visitors, poor innocent taxi-drivers had to attend English classes, and a huge clock, next door to the Central Railway Station, instead of showing the time, indicated how many days ahead the opening of Expo 70 was. Osaka looks forward to it with immense pride and also with dread: the traffic jams will end all traffic jams and the shortage of hotel rooms will be agonising. Already there was not one single hotel room to be had by private individuals for the four pleasant months of Expo, not only in Osaka but also in Kyoto, Nara, Kobe and Tokyo: they had all been booked by airlines or travel agents. (There were some rooms for July and August; and this was the situation eight months before the opening.) But the eyes of the world will be on Osaka and this will compensate for a lot. It is the city's only regret that Tokyo too will benefit, almost equally, in the boom brought by foreign visitors. I am no Expo-man myself and I would not go back to see the great show for toffee; but most people are more adventurous, many millions will see it and there is no doubt that Expo 70 will be terrific on its own terms and will beat all previous Expos. And it will be – as they not infrequently point out – the first World Exposition in Asia.

But Expos come and go. Osaka's moment of glory will pass and the city will have to rely once again not on its momentary catching of the limelight but on its intrinsic fame.

Which is growing at an alarming speed. A Japanese gentleman, an official of the Expo, asked me: 'Is it true that they call Manchester the Osaka of England?'

'Well,' I answered, 'they ought to, of course, but they were always a little slow there up North.'

Ryokan

You will – or anyway you should – stay a few days in a *ryokan*, a Japanese inn. They are usually beautiful and well-run and there you can get closer to real Japanese life than almost anywhere else – except, of course, if you really take the plunge, move to a Japanese fishing village, and mix with what they call the 'people' (as if city-dwellers were not people). But in that village, again, you are likely to stay in a *ryokan*.

You arrive, say, at five p.m. and you get your first dinner early. Pretty, smiling waitresses in *kimonos* will bring in your meal on a tray. You sit on the *tatami*, the exquisitely woven straw-mat, on the floor, wearing your *yukata* and feel that you look like a minor official of the Tokugawa period.

You enjoy the food which is tasty though puzzling. You have no idea in what order you are supposed to eat it and make the foolish and ridiculous mistake of starting with soup.

You finish your dinner, the charming lady – more a hostess than a maid – will come in and within five minutes will transform your room. It will be a complete change of scenery – and scenery is the right word because the whole set-up is slightly yet pleasantly theatrical. The little low table will disappear on to the balcony, two mattresses will be laid out on the *tatami*, one covered with a red, the other with a blue eiderdown. A jug of iced water is placed next to your pillow and a small, weak foot-light is left on, near the door. In the old days six or eight people had to occupy one room (this is not absolutely unknown even today in some remote country districts) and the little light (another piece of stage equipment) was to ensure that the latecomers or early risers would not tread on the others. In some *ryokans* one could not even switch the small light off.

Next morning the scene is changed back: the mattresses disappear and you are delighted with your pretty room until you realise, after lunch, that you cannot lie down anywhere even for ten minutes. Your mattresses are neatly stored in the cupboard and there is just nothing to lie on unless, of course, you lie down on the bare *tatami* – the English equivalent of which would be to put your knife into your mouth and scratch your head with your fork.

The *tatami* is sacred. You will be initiated into the shoe-ceremony on your arrival. On coming home, you take your shoes off and the porter takes charge of them and keeps them for you in his little hut. You step into a pair of lovely, comfortable slippers, always placed in such a way that you should be able to slip your feet straight into them, without touching them with your hands. You use these slippers everywhere in the house, except... except that you must also learn the loo-ceremony. When going to the loo you step out of your ordinary slippers and step into the special loo-slippers, and leaving that establishment you leave the loo-slippers facing the entrance so that the next visitor – probably yourself – will be able to step into them without touching them with his hands. This is regarded as elementary courtesy to yourself. You have also to learn the *tatami*-ceremony: before stepping on the *tatami* you must take your slippers off. There are no special slippers for the *tatami*: you must walk on it in your stockinged feet. The most heinous crime, of course, is to walk on the

tatami wearing your loo-slippers; a crime which – being thoroughly confused by all this changing of slippers – you frequently commit.

You really feel at home in the *ryokan*. They are sweet to you, charming and welcoming. As soon as you come home – and you may return home ten times a day – your own maid will bring you hot towels – a very refreshing and civilised habit – and a pot of green tea which most people love but I detest. The Japanese are as sensitive about their tea as the English, so I invariably poured my tea down the loo (usually wearing my non-loo slippers) because they would have been hurt if I had just left it. The loo itself in my *ryokan* was a Western one with sketches and drawings and written instructions in Japanese, meant for absolute beginners, on how to use it. (The drawings were very neat, showing a gentleman in standing and sitting position, and the text, I was told, was concise and instructive, composed by the Professor of Scatology, Tokyo University.)

The great difficulty in the *ryokan* is communication. Only the lady at the front desk is supposed to know English. A Tokyo friend of mine, a Mr Shirato, promised me that he would come down to see me in Kyoto and would – if he could – stay at my inn. So I went to the front desk, trying to find out if Mr Shirato had booked a room. I asked my question. The lady smiled. I repeated my question. The lady smiled even more charmingly and this time she repeated: 'Mr Shirato.' I nodded. She took the telephone book and rang up three different Mr Shiratos in Kyoto and shook her head sadly. I tried a bit of a charade, pointing to the bedrooms and imitating a man sleeping. She laughed heartily. I pointed to her own list of reservations and asked: 'Mr Shirato?' She looked to see if she had received a message from Mr Shirato, then rang up a fourth Mr Shirato in Kyoto, and finally shook her head more sadly than ever before. Suddenly she had a brainwave. She gave me pencil and paper and indicated that I should draw my question. But how do you draw 'Has Mr Shirato booked a room?'

Soon afterwards I discovered an admirable institution, common to all *ryokans*. Our maid came in with a roneod booklet of Japanese phrases, the English translation written next to them. She pointed to the English question: 'What do you want for breakfast?' I pointed to the Japanese answer: 'Coffee, toast and boiled egg.' She asked with her fingers: 'At what time?' 'Eight thirty,' I pointed, in fluent Japanese.

That little booklet caused one of the bitterest disappointments of my life. One day my pretty maid, wearing her alluring *kimono*, came in and pointed to the question: 'Do you want to see my front?'

I nodded. Yes, I would be very pleased to see her front.

She pointed: 'Please follow me.'

I followed her, not a little surprised and with an air of anticipation. But all she wanted was for me to see her front desk.

The *ryokan* closed its doors at 12 p.m. and there was a large and conspicuous sign at the entrance, in English:

'ALL GUESTS ARE REQUESTED TO BE
UNITED IN BED BEFORE MIDNIGHT'

That was the clearest and most lucid instruction I ever came across in Japan.

Paros, Greece
June-September, 1969